Be Happy Now

Be Happy Now

Simple Steps for Enjoying Life

Laura Barrette Shannon

BALBOA.
PRESS

A DIVISION OF HAY HOUSE

Balboa Press books may be ordered through booksellers or by contacting:

Balboa Press
A Division of Hay House
1663 Liberty Drive
Bloomington, IN 47403
www.balboapress.com
1-(877) 407-4847

Because of the dynamic nature of the Internet, any web addresses or links contained in this book may have changed since publication and may no longer be valid. The views expressed in this work are solely those of the author and do not necessarily reflect the views of the publisher, and the publisher hereby disclaims any responsibility for them.

The author of this book does not dispense medical advice or prescribe the use of any technique as a form of treatment for physical, emotional, or medical problems without the advice of a physician, either directly or indirectly. The intent of the author is only to offer information of a general nature to help you in your quest for emotional and spiritual well-being. In the event you use any of the information in this book for yourself, which is your constitutional right, the author and the publisher assume no responsibility for your actions.

ISBN: 978-1-4525-4800-5 (sc)
ISBN: 978-1-4525-4802-9 (hc)
ISBN: 978-1-4525-4801-2 (e)

Library of Congress Control Number: 2012903836

Any people depicted in stock imagery provided by Thinkstock are models, and such images are being used for illustrative purposes only. Certain stock imagery © Thinkstock.

Printed in the United States of America

Balboa Press rev. date: 3/27/2012

Also by
Laura Barrette Shannon
Awakening Perception: Poetry of a Toltec Warrior (2006)

For my son, Rick.
Your presence gave me the will to transform.

And
in memory of my daughter, Nicole.
Through life and death, you have always been my teacher.

Live with joy and peace by
embracing life as it unfolds,
allowing you to experience who you are.
Accept and appreciate life today,
knowing that you have the power
to transform the future by transforming yourself.

Contents

Preface

This book is the fruit of a tree that has been growing in my mind for over twenty years. The seed was planted long ago in an open mind of turbulent tides. I would often wonder why some people were happy and others were miserable, despite their fortunate circumstances. I was intrigued by my own lack of emotional control, often completely unaware of why I felt the storm of inner angst even though life seemed to be fine.

My emotional instability drew me to dark places, which I tried to hide from the outside world. At the same time, I knew that life was a precious gift. Each downward cycle would be followed by a high cycle. The upswings of emotion would yield extraordinary periods of high accomplishment and an *I can do anything* attitude. For the early part of life, I learned to hide the dark side as best I could and show only my best side. I was an overachiever, taking first place in many science fairs, acing classes with ease, completing the rigorous training of becoming a black belt in Kenpo karate, and basically accomplishing anything I set my mind to do. Then there were the dark periods filled with depression, low energy, disconnected thoughts, weight gain, failing classes, and a lack of passion for life. I was bipolar, as many in my family are, but had yet to realize it or understand it.

It was in the midst of one of these long, downward spirals of depression in 2000 when I found myself unable to work because of physical health issues relating to my brain stem, something called a Chiari malformation. The fact that I was unable to work anymore exacerbated the depression because I felt that I was losing part of my identity. I was in pain all the time, my arms and legs would often go numb, and near the end I had a hard time following conversations. I needed brain surgery to fix the condition.

One month before the surgery, my eleven-year-old daughter died in a traffic accident.

The surgery went on as scheduled, saving my life. The doctor said that the situation was worse than anticipated, because the cerebral spinal sac was herniated. If I had postponed the surgery, the sac may have ruptured. These circumstances—processing the death of my daughter and facing my own mortality—brought about a period of deep soul searching, which began a process of extraordinary personal transformation.

Over the next few years, I came to understand that much of my mental suffering was caused by the way I was thinking and processing the world around me. My thoughts affected my emotions. I learned that what I fed my mind with books, TV, and conversations affected what type of thoughts predominated in my head. So I developed techniques to redirect my attention toward more spiritually uplifting input.

I began to practice meditation and the art of being present. The ability to calm my mind and be present became my salvation. When I was still, I could feel the energy of life thriving around me, through me. The natural world became a source of wonder and joy.

As my awareness grew, I began to awaken, to see that life is perfectly beautiful in its complex duality. Through the darkest tides, our souls are revealed, like the beach at low tide. When we are pushed to our limits of emotional or physical pain, it can be an opportunity to explore what is revealed underneath. I realized that I am not my pain, that I am not my story or my past. I am a living consciousness, an expression of loving energy, a child of life. When I speak of life, I refer to the universal life energy that permeates all things that some call God. It is through the spiritual communion with life that I am able to maintain a higher awareness that enables me to transmute emotions. When I am disconnected from life and from my authentic self, I find myself becoming lost in the emotional tides. I've learned that being who I am, allowing my life to be an expression of my authentic self, promotes a sense of passion and joy with which nothing else compares. The tides of life will come to us all. Life has a rhythm of its own and is always changing in one direction or the other. These tides may seem more pronounced to people like me with bipolar disorder, but we all face them. The lessons and tools I am sharing in this book have helped me to calm the waves and to ride them instead of letting them sweep me up in their momentum.

The purpose of this book is to share the lessons I have learned. By sharing these lessons, others may be able to raise their awareness and rediscover their authentic selves. These lessons are seeds of personal transformation. I may plant the seeds, but only you can make them grow. This is a book of knowledge. As such, you must question everything for yourself, for knowledge is just an interpretation of reality. Wisdom is when you apply the knowledge and find what works for you.

I recommend reading one chapter at a time and then applying the exercises. You will learn more about yourself. Each exercise will gently raise your awareness. If you read the book all at once, then I recommend going back to apply each lesson one at a time. You cannot read a book and become happier. But you can read a book, gain practical knowledge, and then apply it to your life, which in turn may transform you. These are the lessons that worked for me. May you take what works for you, and above all enjoy your journey of awakening to a life of joy and inner peace.

I would like to acknowledge the following people for their contributions to this book: Joan Hartsough for inspiring me to begin the project and for the countless of hours of philosophical discussion about each topic in the book, my brother Jerry Smith for his loving support and guidance, Rosemary Smith for always encouraging my writing and allowing the use of her motto, Angie Hoover Lawson for contributing her wonderful words about being of service to others, Jonathan Lockwood Huie for his powerful happiness quotes, Mark Wainwright, for allowing me to use his "lug nut" analogy for relationships, Debbie Hart, for her unwavering belief in my dream to write this book, Andrea Fenton, for the use of her candid photo for my author picture, my husband Ray Shannon for being so patient and supportive, and especially all of my faithful blog followers on Facebook, your encouragement kept my enthusiasm going.

I would also like to extend my eternal gratitude to the many teachers who have touched my life. This includes all of the people who I have ever known and all whose words have brushed upon my mind, adding to the artistic tapestry of my thoughts.

Be happy, my friends,

Laura Barrette Shannon
Largo, Florida
February 2012

Introduction

"I believe that the very purpose of our life is to seek happiness." ~ *Dalai Lama*

"Happiness is the meaning and the purpose of life, the whole aim and end of human existence." ~ *Aristotle*

Aristotle posed a question over a thousand years ago. He asked, "What is the good life?" The answer is as important today as it was then.

Is the good life ...

having financial independence?
being wealthy?
having a family?
being healthy?
being successful?
being well known?
being loved?
living somewhere beautiful?
being retired?

These are the dreams of many, but do they make people happy? How many times have we seen the drama, stress, and chaos of the rich and famous? How many suicides have we seen by people who were dearly loved by their family and friends? People who appear to have everything going for them are still complaining, still waiting for that magical moment in the future when they will finally be happy.

"When I was five years old my mom always told me that happiness was the key to life. When I went to school they asked me what I wanted to be when I grew up. I wrote down 'happy.' They told me I didn't understand the assignment. I told them they didn't understand life." ~ *John Lennon*

Most of us would probably agree that a happy life is a good life, regardless of the other factors. So if being happy is one of the most important aspects of life, then why is it that we aren't taught how to be happy? Perhaps we never knew that happiness can be taught. Perhaps we are not aware that it is possible to control our emotions or our state of mind. If we took as much time working on happiness, as we do other goals in life, we would all be happy today.

Our culture surrounds us with negative drama. We read it in the newspaper, see it on the nightly news, and hear it from our friends. How can we be surrounded by drama and complaints and still be happy? It's probably hard to believe, but you have everything you need to be happy right now. All you have to do is realize why you feel the way you do.

Some of you might not even know what it means to be happy. I believe happiness is being in love with life. It's when your heart skips a beat when you feel the warmth of sunlight on your face, as well as when the rain wets your hair. Happiness is unconditional love of life. When we allow our happiness to be affected by external sources, we are living with conditional happiness. This type of happiness is temporary and will only be felt when the conditions are just right. Be aware of this way of thinking the next time you feel down or blue. Learn to appreciate life's tides, flowing with each day as it unfolds. Remind yourself that every rainstorm comes to an end and that even the flowers bow their heads in respect, because they know that the storm is for their own growth.

Happiness is beyond being content with life. It is living life with passionate joy mixed with the inner peace of acceptance and appreciation for being alive.

Fall in unconditional love with life. When you love unconditionally, you will overlook the negative and naturally focus on the positive. You will love life no matter what happens.

This book will gently guide you toward a happier state of mind. The causes of unhappiness will be discussed as well as simple steps to bring about peace and happiness in your life.

~ 1 ~

Life Is a Garden

"A man is what he thinks about all day long."
~ Ralph Waldo Emerson

"As a man thinketh in his heart, so is he."
~Proverbs 3:7

Every plant starts with a seed. If you plant dandelion seeds, then dandelions will grow. If you plant daisy seeds, then daisies will grow. Life is the same way. If you plant seeds of unhappiness, then naturally an unhappy life will sprout forth. If you plant seeds of joy, then happiness will naturally grow. But what are these seeds? And how do you plant them? And how can you weed your garden so that you'll have room for joy to grow?

Through a series of simple steps, you will learn how to plant seeds of happiness, take control of your life, weed as necessary, and gain the tools to maintain a garden of joy and happiness.

First, it is important to understand the seeds that we plant. It all begins with our thoughts. Every thought is a seed that will germinate, form roots, and grow. Over time, repetitive thoughts of the same nature tend to grow stronger, supporting each other. This is great if the thoughts are happy and positive, but this is detrimental to your well-being if the thoughts are negative.

In *The Power of Positive Thinking,* Norman Vincent Peale wrote, "Repetition of the same thought or physical action develops into a habit which, repeated frequently enough, becomes an automatic reflex." If you are in a state of unhappiness, it is a result of repetitive unhappy thoughts, which over time have become your natural way of reacting to the world.

Many people aren't even aware of what they are thinking or that their thoughts have so much power over their emotional state. One way to reveal the nature of your thoughts is to watch what you are saying. If most of your conversations revolve around drama and complaints, you probably feel stressed and depressed. Become aware that anything you say out loud first began as a thought in your mind. Speech is a mirror of your mind. Therefore the nature of your speech will either positively or negatively affect your mood.

Lesson #1:

Your thoughts affect your emotions.

Exercise:

This week, start to notice how you are feeling. When you are upset, what are you thinking? When you are happy, what thoughts are on your mind? Begin to understand the relationship between thoughts and emotions. This exercise is about raising your awareness of both your thoughts and your emotions. Nothing else is required other than paying attention to both as much as possible.

~ 2 ~

Happiness Starts Here

"Happiness is not a state to arrive at, but a manner of traveling."
~ Margaret Lee Runbeck

Intent is the seed of creation. Set your intent to have peace of mind and happiness. Without this intent, your mind will develop a million reasons why you shouldn't be happy. The power of intent will keep your mind focused on the goal, not the obstacles, allowing the seed of happiness to grow.

This is where I started. Years ago, I was in a place of personal hell, until I set the intent to become happy and at peace with myself and life. I thought I was a victim of life circumstances. I was physically disabled, battled bipolar swings, and was very unhappy. Then my eleven-year-old daughter died suddenly in a traffic accident. I felt that life was a nightmare and that I was a failure. I felt useless and couldn't stand it anymore.

So one day I set the intent for peace of mind. I cried out to God, who I wasn't sure was listening, and the part of me that did believe He would hear my prayer thought that I must have been long forgotten or being punished. I was lost, but I asked for help. I was powerless to get myself out of this state of hell, so I gave it up to God. I believed that I could be happy, with the help of spirit. It was this moment of desiring peace of mind that planted the seed that would change my life. My state of mind didn't change overnight, but I can tell you that it would never have happened if I didn't believe it was possible, set the intent, and asked for help.

Lesson #2:

Believe that you can live a life of joy and peace. Set the intent to be happy.

Exercise:

Evaluate the way you have been thinking. Do you believe that you will ever be happy? Do you concentrate on why you are not happy? These thoughts will only reinforce your unhappy mind-set.

The first simple step to being happy is to plant the seed. Say this: "I believe that I can live a life of joy and peace."

Or you can pray: "Please, God, show me how to allow more joy and peace into my life."

Repeat these intents as often as necessary, and one day you will realize that you do indeed live a life of happiness.

Remember to be patient with your progress. A flower doesn't grow in one day. But it will never grow if you don't plant the seed. If you believe in a higher power God, pray for peace and happiness for yourself and those around you. What you wish for others is always mirrored back to you. Above all, begin to believe that you can live a life of joy and peace.

~3~

You Have Everything You Need

"Life does not consist mainly, or even largely, of facts and happenings. It consists mainly of the storm of thought that is forever flowing through one's head." ~ Mark Twain

Is happiness something that you believe will come attached to some future event or special person? Are you postponing happiness until you have the ideal job, live in your dream home, find the perfect mate, retire, or have some other future situation? If you find yourself caught up in these thoughts, you will always be waiting for happiness to arrive, which never will, because those types of events will bring only temporary fulfillment.

Don't fall into the trap of delayed happiness! By repeating these types of thoughts, you convince yourself that some outside circumstance or future event will bring happiness. This is one of the biggest lies we tell ourselves. Be happy *now,* because that's really all we ever experience—the present moment. The root of happiness is not connected to the circumstances in your life.

Benjamin Franklin described it like this: "Happiness depends more on the inward disposition of mind than on outward circumstances." If you're not happy now, then you won't be happy no matter what happens in the future unless you change yourself. You hold the key to your own happiness.

The only constant in life is change. Instinctively we know this, so it is only natural to dream of a future aligned with our deepest desires. There will be hopes and dreams along your journey, each one eagerly anticipated as you walk through life. Focusing on these dreams and goals is a healthier mind-set than focusing on the past, yet do not forget to also stay present as much as possible. Enjoy today. These are the good old times that you will talk about someday. Life is what's happening while you're waiting for the future. Experience the journey with joy and awareness, because in the end most destinations are just stepping-stones to bigger dreams.

Not only are life situations not connected to happiness, but neither are people. Other people can't make you happy anymore than we can make other people happy. Happiness is not something that can be given to someone. Happiness is something that we can only give to ourselves.

Many people have fallen into the habit of trying to fill the emptiness, loneliness, and sadness they feel in their lives by thinking they can buy happiness. They become mindless shoppers filling the boredom of their existence with new gadgets, toys, clothes, pocketbooks, shoes, jewelry, or any other thing that fancies them at the time. They look to the excitement of attaining new things to drown the pain of unhappiness in an attempt to bring passion back into their lives. And it seems to actually work, temporarily. The high of the new purchase soon subsides, and the hollowness that they feel inside still remains, so they begin looking for the next new thing to distract them from the real issue. But in reality all they need to do is to activate the happiness within themselves that has been suppressed.

Lesson #3:

You hold the key to your happiness, not special people, new things, or ideal life circumstances.

Exercise:

Is there something that you've been waiting for before you will allow yourself to be happy? Contemplate what those thoughts do to you. Thoughts like that convince yourself that you can't be happy until something happens. Begin to believe that you can be happy regardless of what the future holds. Begin to believe that you have the power be happy *now*. Begin to believe that you hold the key to your own happiness.

This exercise is meant to raise the awareness of your beliefs about what causes happiness. Once you can see that some of your beliefs may be based on false criteria, you will begin to believe that you have everything you need to be happy.

~ 4 ~

Be Present

You cannot own
a shimmering sunset,
or crystal stars of night.
You cannot own
a brilliant blowing breeze,
or the spark of sweet sunlight.

You cannot keep
a fragrant floral scent,
or an infant's sleepy sigh.
You cannot keep
love's first embrace,
or life's ecstatic highs.

So experience enjoyment
in each moment,
immerse in sight, sense, and sound.
Appreciate this world
for all that it is,
that's where abundance is found.

"Abundance" from Awakening Perception

Lesson #1: Your thoughts affect your emotions, brought attention to the powerful relationship between thoughts and emotions. Now that you can see this relationship, you are ready to begin preparing your garden of happiness. One of the most important factors in establishing a thriving garden is to prepare the soil with nutrients. The most important nutrient in a life of happiness is *presence*. Abraham Maslow, the founder of humanistic psychology, maintained that "the ability to be in the present moment is a major component of mental wellness." When you are present, you aren't thinking about the past or the future. The act of being present in any given moment will immediately and effectively break your train of thought, giving you the opportunity to experience the freedom of the moment. Eckhart Tolle described this well when he wrote,

"Unease, anxiety, tension, stress, worry—all forms of fear—are caused by too much future, and not enough presence. Guilt, regret, resentment, grievances, sadness, bitterness, and all forms of non-forgiveness are caused by too much past, and not enough presence" (*The Power of Now*, page 50).

When you are fully present, all that matters is the moment. You aren't dwelling on the past or worrying about the future. Your attention is on the present moment, which enables you to enjoy life like a little child. We all used to live in the *now*. We used to go from activity to activity, never thinking about what happened last week and never worrying about next week. As we aged, we lost our ability to be present. We began to be caught up in our thoughts more than what was happening at the time. Our awareness became trapped in another time, inside our heads, tuning out present life. How can you truly enjoy life if you're not experiencing it? When we are constantly caught up in thoughts, we are not truly living.

When you are enjoying your time, you are present. You're focusing on whatever you are doing without thinking about the past or future. See if you can bring this awareness into your daily activities. The more you practice controlling your attention, the easier it becomes. The more you focus this attention outside your head, the more you will find joy in the simplest things. Be mindful by paying attention to your life as it happens.

The act of being present is an awareness of your surroundings in a new and exciting way. You will appreciate nature, perhaps feeling the sun on your face, hearing the sweet melodies of the birds, or noticing other stimuli that would normally be drowned out by your thoughts. You will enjoy your meals with new vitality, savoring each bite and allowing yourself to taste each flavor. You will become more conscious of your own body, feeling the joy of each breath as it enters and exits your lungs. You will come to realize that the act of being present will draw your mind away from thoughts of the past and worries of the future. All that will matter is *now*, because you will be actively engaging your senses in the present moment.

Being present as much as possible will enliven your life. When you are fully present, your awareness is in a different state of attention. In this state of attention, you are aware of your present moment of activity and you are also aware of your thoughts. Many people are in a constant state of unawareness. They will go about their days rarely being present and barely aware of their surroundings and what they are thinking. More often than not, they don't understand why their emotions are out of control.

Allow yourself to experience the small pleasures of life. It's through enjoying the most ordinary moments that we begin to live. In reality, life is just a string of very ordinary moments. By enjoying the day-to-day happenings, you are learning to enjoy life.

Lesson #4:

You have the ability to bring your attention to the present moment.

Exercise:

Practice controlling your attention by being present.

Choose at least one activity that you normally do every day. It can be anything at all: eating, showering, drinking coffee, exercising, etc. Whenever you do this activity, be present as much as possible. Start by bringing your attention to your body and senses. What do you feel physically? What do you see, smell, and hear? At the same time, be aware of your thoughts. It's natural to have thoughts. The goal isn't to eliminate them but to let them pass by like trains in a train station.

Examples:

Walking. Be aware of the physical sensations; feel your muscles contract as you walk. Feel the heat or cold on your skin. Feel the textures of your clothing. Be aware of any sounds; listen to the sound of your own breath as it flows in and out.

Eating. Take time to enjoy the taste and aroma of your food. Savor each bite as if you never tasted it before. Pay attention to the texture, the way your tongue moves as you chew.

Really focus on staying present. When you find your mind drifting to other thoughts, gently pull yourself back into the moment. This exercise will demonstrate just how much you are caught up in your thoughts versus being present. Be a human *being,* not a human *thinking.*

Be where you are.

Do what you are doing.

Experience life as it happens.

When we live inside our heads, thinking about being somewhere else, doing something else, or thinking about the past or the future, we are missing out on living. You will enjoy life more if you actually live it as it unfolds.

Don't judge your efforts. Even if you can only be present for five seconds at a time, you have successfully begun your journey toward being happy now.

~ 5 ~

Breathe

In this world of chaotic change,
I Am at peace.
Breath of tranquility
Calms my restless mind.
Just being Present
Blocks emotional turmoil,
Reminding me
What is Real.

"What Is Real" from Awakening Perception

Everyone breathes. Most of us breathe unconsciously, allowing our autonomic nervous systems to regulate the depth and rhythm of each inhale and exhale. There are many benefits to taking control of your breathing, whether it is for one slow, deep breath or longer deep-breathing exercises.

"Deep breathing techniques increase oxygen to the cells and are the most important factors in living a disease-free and energetic life." ~Dr. Otto Warburg, the president of the Institute of Cell Physiology and two-time winner of the Nobel Prize for Medicine.

Besides the overall physical benefits of deep breathing, it is also advantageous in developing our ability to respond to life instead of to react. One slow, deep breath is enough to refocus your attention away from your thoughts and into your body. This is a priceless tool for redirecting attention as well as relieving tension. Learning to take one or two slow, deep breaths is the beginning of taking control of your emotions.

The ABCs of redirecting attention:

A – Awareness. When you become aware of a negative emotion, you have gained the personal power to respond instead of to react.

B – Breathe. Take a few slow, deep breaths. Feel the air move in and out of your body. Feel your muscles. Relax. This switches your awareness away from the charged emotion and into your body and the present moment.

C – Choose. Now that you have taken a moment to calm the emotion, you have the ability to choose an appropriate response.

Use the ABCs of redirecting attention, and you will feel less stressed and have more control of how you act and speak.

We can use breathing exercises in many ways. One that I use is taking a slow, deep breath when I feel a twinge of irritation. An example is when I spill something all over my desk. I will feel a brief moment of agitation, and then I will take a deep breath, which allows the emotion to pass through my body and exit with the exhale. This allows me to move forward with my day without carrying the residual negative emotion from the event. Most stress is caused by a buildup of numerous minor irritations throughout the day. When we consciously breathe, it refocuses our attention on the present moment, which effectively breaks our train of thought. This is an invaluable tool for transformation, and it is one of the most effective ways to avoid stress building up inside you.

Lesson #5:

Consciously breathing is one of the most important tools for self-awareness, transformation, and stress relief.

Exercise:

Deep breathing can also be used for relaxation and physical well-being. Try the following simple breathing exercise.

1. Inhale slowly to the count of five, filling your lungs as much as possible. Feel your lungs expand. Visualize healing energy coming into your body.
2. Hold the breath for a count of three.
3. Exhale slowly to the count of five, squeezing every bit of air out. Feel your muscles contract to expel the air. Visualize releasing toxins from your body.
4. Hold for the count of three.
5. Repeat at least ten times.
6. For a more advanced technique, slow the inhale and exhale to a higher count.

Relax, breathe deeply, and be happy.

~ 6 ~

The Worried Woman

There once was a woman who had two sons. The first son was a farmer and the second was a brick maker. During the rainy season, she lamented and cried because the brick maker couldn't make his bricks. During the dry season, she complained and worried that her son's crops would dry up and burn. Every day she would be worried about one son or the other.

One day a wise old monk came to town. The worried woman asked the wise monk how she could find peace and happiness when each day she was worried about one of her sons. The wise monk said, "On the days of rain, rejoice! For your son's crops are being blessed with water to yield a plentiful harvest! On the days of sun, rejoice! For the heat of the sun is baking down on your son's bricks, allowing him to be more productive in his brick-making business." From that day forward, the woman was happy every day. (This is the retelling of an old Buddhist tale.)

Lesson #6:

What you focus on affects your level of happiness or misery.

Exercise:

Start to evaluate the nature of the things you talk and think about. See if you can notice when you are focusing on negative life situations or worries. When we pay too much attention to things that are upsetting, and usually out of our control, we are upsetting ourselves for no reason. This is an awareness exercise. You don't need to change your habits of thinking at this time; just become aware that what you focus on affects your level of happiness or misery.

~ 7 ~

Trains of Thought

"The greater part of human pain is unnecessary. It is self-created as long as the unobserved mind runs your life." ~ Eckhart Tolle

Thoughts are like trains passing through your mind. You can either let the train go by, silently watching it flow through, or you can jump on the train of thought, allowing it to bring you to a destination. Some trains go to happy places: warm memories, future dreams, gratitude, present surroundings. Others go to places of misery: regret, worry, resentment, complaints. Be aware of what train you jump on. When you pay attention to trains of thought, they grow stronger and come more often. Begin to be aware of how your thoughts affect your moods. Ask yourself, "Where is this train going?" Then you can either stay on it or jump off!

The optimal goal is not to allow ourselves to indulge in trains of thought that lead to misery and suffering. But since this takes time to master, most of us will occasionally find ourselves on a self-destructing train of thought. To maintain peace of mind, we must learn how to jump from negative trains to happy trains.

There are many ways to change your train of thought. One of the easiest is to bring your awareness back to the present moment. Use the ABCs of redirecting attention. Take one or two slow, deep breaths. Pay attention to your surroundings; concentrate on feeling your body sensations, sights, sounds, and smells. When you are fully present, your mind will not be thinking about past trauma, today's complaints, or tomorrow's worries. You will be in the now, fully aware and free to experience life outside your head until you jump onto a more pleasant train of thought. Practice being aware of what train you are riding, and jump trains as necessary. The more you practice, the easier it will be, until one day it will be second nature. The less attention you pay to the negative trains of thought, the less often they will come to mind and the quicker they will pass through, eventually not coming much at all.

Lesson #7:

By redirecting your attention, you have the ability to jump off negative trains of thought.

Exercise:

Practice jumping trains of thought.

When you become aware that you are riding on a negative train of thought, jump off. Practice bringing your awareness back to the present moment. Take a slow, deep breath. Engage in the sensory input around you. Stay present as long as possible. Engage in your life as it is unfolding before you. Become an active participant in your surroundings. Eventually, pick a happier train of thought to ride. Choose trains like gratitude, future dreams, or compassion.

Be gentle with yourself during this training phase. You've spent a lifetime riding on the same unhappy trains over and over. It will take some time to lay new train tracks. Any amount of effort you give this exercise will pay off more than you realize.

~ 8 ~

Acceptance

"God, grant me the serenity
to accept the things I cannot change;
courage to change the things I can;
and wisdom to know the difference."
~ Reinhold Niebuhr

One of the most essential happy seeds to plant in your life is acceptance. When we cultivate acceptance, it will begin to strangle the weeds of discontent. You've probably heard the saying, "It is what it is." When we can begin to accept that certain things in life are beyond our control, then we can understand the uselessness of complaining about them. Living with acceptance doesn't mean that you condone the imperfections of this world. It means that you have chosen to see beyond them in order to allow yourself to enjoy life.

Acceptance is a fundamental seed of happiness. Before we can plant this seed, we must admit that sometimes life involves events that we cannot control. Realize that accepting something doesn't necessarily mean that you like what happened; it is admitting that the past happened as it did and releasing the thoughts of wishing it had been different. You can never change the past, but you can move forward without fighting it. You cannot move forward until you are willing to let the past go.

Besides accepting the past, you must learn to accept the present. When you allow yourself to get caught up in conversations that are focused on complaining about current events, you are filling your mind with seeds of misery. Be aware of focusing too much on what is wrong with the world. When you focus on obstacles and problems, you fail to see solutions. Happy people look beyond life's imperfections and do not talk about them all day.

Now that you've awakened your ability to be present at will and know that you can be happy now, you are ready to begin exploring your life, weeding as necessary and planting new seeds of joy. Lesson #4: You have the ability to bring your attention to the present moment, taught that you can control your attention. You successfully practiced redirecting your attention and actively engaging the present moment. This may seem like a small accomplishment, and you are probably wondering how being present will help to transform your life. It's simple. The more you practice being present and being aware of your thoughts, the easier it will be to focus your attention, thereby gaining the ability to jump off negative trains of thought. This gives you the ability to start to really enjoy life.

When you learn to focus your attention at will, you will be able to steer your trains of thought toward more desirable emotions. Thus, by directing your attention, you have unlocked the door to happiness. Happy people have learned to do this, even if they don't know what they are doing. Happy people focus on their flower garden; they pay attention to and nurture the seeds of happiness and do not allow weeds of discontent into their lives.

Lesson #8:

Life won't always be what you think it should be. Accept it anyway.

Exercise:

Is there something you feel you cannot accept? Is it something that you can change? If it is beyond your scope of influence, then it is something that you either must come to accept or continue letting the thoughts of nonacceptance cause you misery.

Become aware of any issues you may have with acceptance. When you find something that is troubling you that you have no control over, plant new seeds of acceptance by repeating the following:

"I may not like _____, but since there is nothing I can do about it, I choose to let these thoughts go."

The more awareness you bring to this issue, the quicker you will be able to stop riding these disturbing trains of thought. Eventually they will come less and less. Be gentle with yourself as you learn to accept that life won't always be what you think it should be.

~ 9 ~

Complaints Are Seeds of Misery

Life is a flower garden,
your thoughts are the seeds.
You'll reap what you sow,
plant flowers not weeds.
Accept what is—
allow life to flow!
Speak only delight
Wherever you go!
~LB Shannon

When we cultivate acceptance, it will begin to strangle the weeds of discontent. When we can begin to accept that certain things in life are beyond our control, then we can understand the uselessness of complaining about them. When we complain, we are planting seeds of misery in our minds and spreading those seeds to other people.

Complaining will amplify your fixation on negative circumstances. If you can change what you are wishing to change, then have the courage to do it. If you choose not to, then stop complaining. If it is something beyond your control, then the complaining serves only one purpose: to aggravate yourself and others around you.

Not only is complaining a waste of time and energy, but it is detrimental to peace of mind. Whenever you complain, you are planting weeds of misery instead of seeds of happiness. You are reinforcing negative thinking with every complaint you utter. Begin to notice how you feel irritated when you complain about things. This irritation is one of the root causes of stress in your life. Stress is caused when the mind refuses to accept what is. When we are constantly dwelling on things that are out of our control, we plant seeds of discontent and anger. The events in our life do not create stress; *our thoughts about these events are the seeds of discontent.*

Mom was right: "If you don't have anything nice to say, then don't say anything at all." Become aware of how your words affect your emotions and those who hear them. It's not just gossip that hurts; it is any complaint or negative comments about life in general. Become aware of the power of your words. Words are powerful. They can bring people together or drive them apart. Watch your words and those around you. Begin to see the power behind them. Practice being positive and you will not only feel better yourself, you will be a light to those around you.

Lesson #9:

Become aware that complaining is a seed of discontent and unhappiness.

Exercise:

Begin to be aware of what you say. Your words are a mirror of your mind. See if you can notice how much you complain and how others will complain about the littlest things. Become aware of what type of conversations you have with people. Are most of your conversations positive and uplifting, or are they mostly complaining about people or life in general? Begin to notice how you feel when you complain about things. How do you feel when others are complaining? All that is required is for you to become aware of how complaining is contributing to your level of stress.

This is an awareness exercise. Raising your awareness is the first step to complaining less. Awareness is the key to getting your emotions under control. Don't judge yourself. Be grateful that you are becoming aware of how stress originates and that you have the power to begin living peacefully.

~ 10 ~

Enjoy Your Own Life

A married woman tending her garden sees a plane go by and dreams of travel. The traveling salesman on the plane sits next to an old man, which starts him dreaming of retirement. The retired old man sitting across from a young family yearns to be young again. The young mother is looking at the teenager sitting in front of her and can't wait for her toddler to be self-sufficient. The teen is looking out the window at the woman in her garden and wishes she was older so she could get married and have her own garden.

We often look away from where we are to the past, the future, or to what someone else has that we think we might enjoy, instead of being where we are in life. The grass isn't any greener anywhere else. Life is what *you* experience. Enjoy your own life instead of wishing you were someone else or in a different time in your life. Each part of your life will be different from the others, but each is worth experiencing while it is here. Whether you are young, old, single, married, traveling, or being a homebody, appreciate it.

Lesson #10:

You can't enjoy life if you are wishing you were someone else or focusing on a different time in your life.

Exercise:

Become aware when you are wishing you were in a different phase of your life. This train of thought devalues where you are right now in life. If you find yourself caught up in *time travel* thinking, bring your awareness back to the present. Begin to focus on gratitude and appreciation for where you are right now in life.

Acting Instead of Re-Acting

"You will not be punished for your anger; you will
be punished by your anger." ~ Buddha

Now that you have become aware of the relationship between complaining and stress, you are ready to learn how to stop complaining and learn to respond to life in a different way. Most complaints are merely reactions that we have learned and practiced over a lifetime. We were never taught how to watch our thoughts. We never knew that there was a different way of looking at life.

The difference between reacting and acting is bringing awareness to the situation. This allows you to use your free will to respond any way you choose. When you react to a situation, you are most likely repeating patterns of behavior without thought to whether your reactions are appropriate for this new situation. You are literally *re*-acting, or acting again, the way you have acted before. When you respond with action to a situation, you are consciously aware of what you are thinking, saying, and doing.

When a stressful situation arises, unhappy people will automatically react with negative thoughts, most of which are resisting the reality of what is. If you are unaware of your thoughts, you have no control over your reactions to life. By taking a moment to be present, you will gain awareness of your thoughts, which will give you an opportunity to choose your response instead of just reacting to the situation. You will act with awareness instead of reacting.

Let's look at an example of the typical unhappy person reacting to a flat tire. The tire blows. Ms. Grimm starts cursing. "I can't believe this!

Now I'm going to be late! This is terrible!" After she hurriedly scrambles to find the number for roadside assistance, she calls with aggravation in her voice. She will spend the time waiting, repeating negative thoughts of nonacceptance, feeling like a victim, and possibly even calling other people to express her irritation, spreading the seeds of misery. Then she will most likely repeat the story of this event multiple times throughout the day, each time becoming upset and feeling stressed.

Now let's see how Ms. Chipper handles the same situation: The tire blows. "Darn!" (Slow, deep breathe.) "Well, I guess I'll call roadside assistance. There's nothing else I can do about it." Keeps breathing deeply and slowly as she calmly calls for assistance. Then starts to think, *Boy, am I thankful that I didn't have an accident when the tire blew! Thank God! I'll call work and let them know I'm going to be late. And now I can call a few people that I've been meaning to call while I wait.* She might repeat this story but will definitely tell it without negative residual emotions.

You may have had the good fortune to witness the difference between an unhappy person and a happy person in a situation. The unhappy people are always stressing themselves out and have a hard time coping when unexpected things happen. The happy people are the ones who are calm and flow with life. The flat-tire incident is a relatively big event compared to the many smaller things that pass our way in any given day. *Most of the time, the events that stress people out are very small.*

Let's look at another example of unchecked thoughts, this time with something small happening. Mr. Grimm is getting ready for work. He isn't thinking about what he is doing and spills coffee on his shirt. Cursing, he starts to rush around. As he is hurrying, he is thinking how clumsy he was for spilling the coffee and how he is going to be late. These thoughts agitate him even more. While he is driving to work he's still thinking about being late and not really focusing on the road. Each red light he stops at aggravates him more and more, which starts him thinking about how much he hates traffic and driving. By the time Mr. Grimm gets to work, he's in a bad mood and is grumpy to everyone he passes on the way to his desk. He has a stressful morning because everything seems to bother him. He starts to think about how much he hates his job. By afternoon, he is feeling stressed and depressed.

Sometimes a tiny event can spiral into a bad mood or even a bad day. Mr. Grimm didn't let the emotions process quickly and in a healthy manner. So he feels irritated while trying to find another shirt, thinking about how he's going to be late, driving faster to work, and getting more irritated at every stop light. By the time he reaches work, a small spill on his shirt has become the trigger for ruining his mood for the morning. He is unaware why he is in a bad mood. He just thinks he is having a bad day.

Now, let's look at an example of catching your thoughts in the same situation. Mr. Chipper is getting ready for work. He isn't thinking about what he's doing and spills coffee on his shirt. "Oops!" (Momentary irritation. Takes a slow, deep breath) "Guess I missed my mouth! (Chuckles.) "I'll go change my shirt." (Feels no residual irritation about this event.) Then he starts to think, *Darn, I'm going to be late now.* Mr. Chipper, recognizing his reaction as a negative thought process, starts to watch his thoughts. He knows what can happen if he lets them run amok. Instead of getting upset, he thinks about having an opportunity to slow down a bit and focus on the present moment. He takes an extra three minutes to change his shirt and leaves for work. He is still focused on the moment and what he is thinking about, so as he drives to work he doesn't rush but enjoys the twenty-minute commute, singing to the music on the radio. He focuses on driving and singing. He happily greets everyone as he enters work and has a great day.

You can see from these very simplistic examples how one thought can trigger other thoughts and create a spiral of emotion. If you can catch your negative thoughts and change them toward something different, or just release them and move on with your day, you will be taking a huge step toward improving your life. These practices take time and effort, but the more you watch your thoughts, the easier it is to see them and not let them take over your emotions.

When we react to every slight irritation all day long, the stress builds inside us. By resisting the flow of life, we condemn ourselves into a life of aggravation. It doesn't have to be that way! You can learn to respond to life in a different way.

Here is where you can use presence. When an unexpected event pops into your day, remember your ABCs. Take a deep breath and let it out slowly. This is exactly the amount of time it takes to let the momentary irritation pass through you and to become present. It's okay to feel the irritation, but let it flow quickly and then let it go.

If you have enough presence, you will be able to stop your train of thought about whatever is bothering you. These few seconds will allow you to inhibit your emotional impulse and evaluate the situation. If it is something that you have no control over, then instead of complaining, (either in your thoughts or out loud) switch your perspective to one of acceptance. You might even remind yourself that it isn't worth getting upset over the issue.

In his book *Emotional Intelligence,* psychologist Daniel Goleman formulates the skills necessary for emotional well-being. He writes,

> "Emotional intelligence consists of five skills: knowing what you're thinking as you're thinking it; handling your feelings so that distracting emotions don't interfere with your ability to concentrate and learn; motivating yourself, including maintaining optimism and hope; having empathy; and social skills."

When you can develop enough awareness to know what you are thinking, and thereby respond to life in a positive way, instead of reacting you are on your way to being an emotionally balanced person. If you can make a habit of this, you'll notice a remarkable change in your life. As a matter of fact, if this is the only lesson you ever apply from this book, then you will have the tools to eliminate stress.

When we complain about life, people, traffic, weather, or life in general, we're not only planting weeds in our garden, we are spreading seeds of misery into someone else's garden. Stop aggravating yourself and everyone around you with complaints!

Lesson #11:

You can respond to life in a positive way. (Stop complaining.)

Exercise:

This week, make an effort to focus your attention on being present and choosing to act with awareness instead of reacting to all the little things that happen in a day. Really make an effort to stop complaining out loud. The negative thoughts will still arise in your mind, but if you have enough awareness to stop those negative thoughts from being spoken, then you are making progress. Eventually, with practice it will become easier and easier to let those negative thoughts flow through your mind before they grab your attention and irritate you.

Don't judge your efforts. Even if you cannot catch yourself before you complain, but do have enough awareness to notice it after you said it, you are making a step toward being a happier person. With enough practice, you will begin to raise your level of awareness, which will enable you to respond positively instead of negatively to life.

Also, practice focusing on the positive aspects of life. Make an effort to talk about uplifting and positive topics of conversation. This will not only improve your mood, but it will help raise the moods of others around you. You can be a positive influence on yourself and others!

~12~

You Are the Narrator of Your Life

"Your living is determined not so much by what life brings to you as by the attitude you bring to life; not so much by what happens to you as by the way your mind looks at what happens." ~ Kahlil Gibran

Your story is what you tell yourself and others about your life. We do this all the time when we meet new people. The longer we know them, the more we fill in our life story with whole chapters and characters we have met. The key is to know that *you* are telling the story, so you have the power to change the viewpoint of the narration.

You are the narrator of your life. Begin watching how you talk about yourself. Your every word defines who you want the world to see and reinforces how you think of yourself. If you keep the narration focused on unlimited potential for the future, lessons from past adversity, appreciation for the people who come and go, and gratitude for life itself, you will not only enjoy life more, you will be a joy to be around. Be a light in your own life, be your own best cheerleader, and watch your life be transformed.

Is your story one of being a victim of circumstance, or is it one of triumph through adversity? Recognize that either version of the story is just a different perspective of the same past events. For example, I could tell my story from a negative point of view ...

I became physically and mentally disabled in my late twenties and early thirties. I went through an emotionally crushing divorce in that same time period. My condition eventually required brain surgery when I was thirty-three. One month before the brain surgery, my eleven-year-old daughter was tragically killed in an accident because some jerk cut them off on the highway. My life has been destroyed by things out of my control. How can I ever be happy? I have to deal with disabling health issues every day, which further makes my life sad and depressing. Life sucks!*

This is a *Woe is me!* type story of victimization.

Or I can tell my story with positive passion ...

Many years ago, I went through some emotional and physical trauma. These events provided an atmosphere of deep introspection of life and were a catalyst for self-transformation. I learned that I can be happy no matter what my past was, my current life circumstances are, or whatever the future holds. I am grateful for my past, because it has given me the opportunity to grow into who I am today.

This is a *Life is good!* type story.

It is important to understand that both versions of the story are just different perspectives of the same past events. The past hasn't changed; the way I look at it has changed. What I choose to emphasize has changed. This switch from a negative perspective into a positive one changed my life.

The choice in how you see and tell your story will affect your self-image and how others see you. Don't play the victim in your life story, and you won't feel like a victim.

Today ask yourself, "What's my story?" If you don't like the story, then change it. Don't fabricate lies, just re-frame how you describe past events and who you are. If you had past adversity or tragedy, begin to speak only of the lessons you have learned. Don't focus on the pain. Focus on how you used the experience to grow as a person or how you learned more about yourself and life. If you can't quite tell it in a positive fashion yet, then do not tell it at all! You write your own story. Make it a happy one.

Lesson #12:

You are the narrator of your life story. Make it a happy one!

33

Exercises:

Take time to sit down and rewrite your life story. It may take many rewrites before you eliminate all of the negative narration that you have been accustomed to telling yourself and others. At least start with one happier, more positive version of your story. You will be able to rewrite it as often and as much as you desire. There are numerous ways to tell any story. Make yours a happy one, even if you don't believe it yet. Until you rewrite your life story into a happy one, refrain from telling it.

Watch how you talk about yourself and what you say about your life story. Story lines to *avoid* are the following:

"I can't do that."

"I'm not good at _____"

"I'm not good enough."

"I feel like a victim of life circumstances."

"I feel like a victim of past events."

"Life is difficult."

"I'll never be happy because _____."

"I'll be happy when _____."

You get the idea. Watch what you say about yourself and your life. Argue for your limitations, and you will always be right. Tell stories of victimization, and you play the part of victim.

Begin to use story lines that cast you as the hero.

"I learned so much going through _____. I am truly grateful for the experience."

"Going through the loss of _____ really taught me how I should never take things for granted."

"I learned that I can grow stronger through adversity."

"I am not afraid to follow my dreams, because I know that failure is just a step on the path and another notch in my belt of experience."

"I know I can be happy no matter what happens in my life."

"Life is good!"

"I chose not to see myself as a victim of past circumstances but a student of life. If I didn't learn something, then that would be a real tragedy."

You are the narrator and the director and can cast yourself as any part you wish in your life story.

Advanced Exercise:

Moving beyond Your Story

Who would you be without your story? When you define yourself by your life story, you are still limiting yourself. You are more than your past, no matter how delightful, painful, exciting, or dramatic it has been. You are just a character in the story, not the story itself. It can be tempting, when people ask who you are, to start telling your life story. The next time someone asks you to share about yourself, tell them your dreams, your values, and what sparks your passion. It's not who you were yesterday that matters; it's who you choose to be now and tomorrow.

~ 13 ~

Don't Play the Victim

"What poison is to food, self pity is to life."
~ Oliver C. Wilson

*"Self-pity is our worst enemy and if we yield to it, we
can never do anything wise in this world."*
~ Helen Keller

Now that you have a firm understanding of the relationship between words and emotions, it is time to look at what you talk about more closely. The focus of this chapter is on raising awareness of how people victimize themselves. What does it mean to victimize yourself? And why would anyone in his or her right mind do such a thing? Unfortunately, people do it all the time and don't even know they are doing it.

When you experience a negative event in your life, it can be very tempting to dwell on it in your thoughts or tell the story over and over days, months, and even many years later. Each time you do this, you are emotionally right back in the situation. Maybe it was someone who physically hurt you, a tragedy, or emotional pain that you tend to revisit time and again. When you rehash old wounds by telling the story again, you reopen them, causing emotional pain. Humans are the only animals on earth that allow themselves to repetitively suffer by the same event. By focusing on when you felt victimized, you are playing the role of the victim once again. This is emotional abuse that you inflict on yourself.

The first time you may be a victim, but the second time you are a volunteer. This is often said about physical abuse when referring to the people who return to harmful situations. When we play the victim, by repeating stories of our perceived victimization we are reinforcing a victim attitude in ourselves. Being a victim will convince you that you are powerless, that life is beyond your control. This is not true. You are only a victim if you believe that you are. You cannot always choose what happens to you in life, but you can choose how to respond to life. Do not play a victim. Take your power back.

If you find yourself caught up in self-pity, immediately bring your awareness back to the present moment. Focus your attention on your physical sensations. Take a deep breath. Actively switch your attention away from thoughts of the past. If you have been in a habit of dwelling on past negative situations, you have not made peace with those situations or the people involved. Until you resolve the issues, they will continue to haunt you. The first step is to stop repetitively verbalizing your past pain to other people.

How do you make peace with your past? It all starts with intent. Begin with the intent that *you can and will be able to live a happy life even though some things happened in the past that you wish did not happen.*

There are many processes for accepting the past and letting the emotions finally flow through you and leave. One of the best I've used is journaling. You can get it all out on paper. Write the things that you might never say to anyone else. Then burn it.

Another method is to tell it to God. Pray for peace of mind and the strength to let it go. Or tell it to your dog, cat, plant, or a candle. Get it all out one final time. Allow yourself to feel the emotions, cry, yell, jump up and down, and release the anger, pain, and sadness. Allow the emotions to fully emerge and to finally be released from your mind and body.

Then, let it go. Repeat it no more. If it comes across your mind, immediately switch your train of thought and don't ride that train. Without your attention, the train will come by less and less, and eventually it won't even pass by. By focusing less on the past pain, you will be taking its emotional fuel away. This will allow you to recover enough personal power to work on acceptance and forgiveness as time passes.

Watch what you say about yourself. When you repeat stories of being a victim, express self-pity, or talk down about yourself, you are giving away your personal power and playing the role of the unworthy victim again and again. Remember lesson #12: You are the narrator of your life story.

Lesson #13:

Be aware of how you talk about yourself. Words can either be empowering or victimizing.

Exercise:

Become aware of how you feel when you repeat stories of victimization. Avoid retelling any story that makes you feel upset or weak. Also, avoid encouraging others to tell their stories of victimization. Avoid saying self-effacing comments, such as, "I'm not good enough, smart enough, or attractive enough." Don't victimize yourself!

If there are issues that still remain emotionally unresolved, please take whatever action is necessary to release the resentment and anger. Don't be afraid to seek professional help, such as a counselor, a psychologist, group counseling, or spiritual guidance. It is time to resolve any issues that make you feel like a victim so you can move forward into a life of joy and peace.

~ 14 ~

The World Is a Mirror

"Judge not, that ye be not judged. For with what judgment ye judge, ye shall be judged: and with what measure ye mete, it shall be measured to you again. And why behold thou the mote that is in thy brother's eye, but consider not the beam that is in thine own eye?" ~ Mathew 7: 1-3

Most of us have heard the above warning about judging, yet many do not really understand the deeper meaning. When we judge others with our criticism and condemnations we are expressing our beliefs about ourselves. For example, if you are disgusted when you see overweight people wearing tight clothing, you have issues within yourself about being overweight or being seen by others in unflattering clothing. If you tend to nitpick the world, always seeing every little thing that is wrong, you will have these same feelings about yourself, never being satisfied with who you are. The world is a mirror. What you see is a reflection of your beliefs. You cannot change the reflection in the mirror unless you change yourself. Be aware of this valuable tool of self-introspection. The better you understand yourself and why you act and see things the way you do, the more awareness and personal power you will have for self-transformation.

Using good judgment is a necessary part of life. Good judgment is when you decide whether to take an umbrella or not on a cloudy day or judge the timing of the cars before you cross the street. The type of judgment that is destructive is when the judgment involves self-righteous attitudes, condemnation, and contempt. These types of thoughts are harmful to yourself and others.

Judging others plants seeds of misery, but be aware that self judgment also leads to emotional suffering. When we chastise ourselves, it lowers our self-esteem and leaves a feeling of sadness. All judgments start within ourselves. Often, our outer judgments and criticisms are reflections of the same judge that speaks inside our heads. Be gentle and accepting with yourself, and the same acceptance is extended to others, and, vice versa- start to be more tolerant and accepting of others, and you will be less critical of yourself. These are important concepts for raising self awareness and discovering why we say or think the things we do. With awareness comes choice, and the ability to change.

It is when we can allow others to err and not focus on their imperfections that we release our self-judgment. By being more tolerant of others, we begin to be more tolerant of our own shortcomings. Just like you, most people are doing the best they can with the state of mind they have in any given moment. Everyone has his or her own personal battles. Knowing this allows feelings of compassion to rise within you. Be kind to others, and you will be kinder to yourself.

When we make assumptions about people by the way they dress, their occupations, levels of education, hairstyles, or any other labels we place upon them, we are deluding ourselves into believing stories about them. This happens all the time. We see the world through the perceptions of our own limited beliefs. Become aware of the tendency to judge a book by its cover, and be open minded and tolerant of others who may be different from yourself. When we release the habit of judging others, we free ourselves in the process.

To err is human. To forgive gives peace of mind. When we make mistakes, we need to be gentle with ourselves. Don't dwell on it with thoughts of self-judgment. Forgive yourself for being human. Learn from your mistakes, and do your best not to repeat them. All forgiveness starts with the self. If we can't forgive ourselves, how can we begin forgive others?

It can be challenging to overcome a lifetime of self-judgment. Be patient with yourself. I use a positive affirmation every morning to remind myself "I love who I am, and who I am becoming." Whenever I feel self-doubt, I repeat this phrase a few times. It may sound like it won't make a difference, but I assure you that it will. Loving yourself first is a fundamental step to being happy.

Lesson #14:

The world is a mirror. To change the way you see others, you must change the way you see yourself.

Exercise:

Become aware of judgmental thoughts you may have about others and yourself. At the very least, stop yourself from voicing the judgments out loud. Eventually, as you practice more acceptance and less judging, the judgmental thoughts will come less and less. If you catch yourself judging others because they are different, ask, "Why not?" instead of "Why?" Remind yourself that people are doing the best they can with the state of mind that they are in at the time. Forgive them for being human and not always making the choices that you would make. By allowing others to be who they are, you are giving yourself that same right.

Stand in front of a mirror and repeat this affirmation:

"I see you, embrace you, and love who you are now and who you are becoming."

The more you learn to accept yourself, despite your imperfections, the more you will accept others. No one is perfect, but by seeing the beauty in the imperfection you will be able to release judgmental thoughts and embrace the light in others.

~ 15 ~

Realize Your Worth

"Be more concerned with your character than with your reputation. Your character is what you really are, while your reputation is merely what others think you are."
~ *John Wooden*

Self-worth should not be defined by your level of education, income, or career. Instead, let your self-worth be linked to good character, compassion, and how much love you spread in the world. It's not what you do for a living; it is who you are that matters. Don't try to compete with other people, evaluating your life based on what others have achieved. The greatest achievement is when we can honestly say that we have done our best to be the best person that we can be.

I learned this lesson in 1999 when I had to stop working because of health issues. It made me reevaluate my self-worth; up until then I had built myself up on my accomplishments and career. This was false self-worth, since it could be taken away. Now I build my worth from the inside, which can never be taken unless I take it from myself. When we allow our self-worth to be tied to outside approval, we set ourselves up for disappointment. Let your path be one with a strong sense of self-worth and you will be free of outside opinions and self-judgment. Plus, you will have more confidence to be yourself.

It can be challenging to see ourselves without the labels and boxes that society uses to define us. When we place more emphasis on who we are as people rather than the roles we play, our self-worth becomes an integral part of who we are. This is true self-esteem. Simply be worthy by being worthy!

Don't get caught up in judging your self-worth by the distorted representations of beauty that the media portrays. Real beauty comes in all shapes, sizes, colors, and cultures. There is nothing more attractive than self-confidence mixed with compassion. Embrace the real beauty of your unique physical characteristics. There is no need to change or hide anything. Have the courage to be yourself, and it will raise your self-worth. Whether you are fluffy or thin, wrinkle free or etched to perfection, be comfortable with yourself.

Do you find it hard to accept a compliment? When we shy away from compliments, uttering something to diminish the praise or even negate it, we are showing and reinforcing our lack of self-worth. Practice responding with a self-confident smile and replying with a genuine "Thank you." You are an amazing person! Let others acknowledge this when they experience your praiseworthy qualities.

Are you a people pleaser? Is it important that people approve of your life and actions? Do you gauge your self-worth by what other people think about you? If you are constantly trying to be the person other people think you should be, then you are not being true to yourself. Stop trying to please everyone. Be yourself, not someone else's idea of who you should be. By being true to who you are and and taking responsibility for your life, you will automatically feel better about yourself, thus raising your sense of self worth.

Learn to love yourself. You should know that you deserve your own love and admiration. You are worthy of a love as strong as you have ever loved anyone else. You are perfect in this moment, even if you desire to make a new definition of perfection tomorrow. Love yourself now, fully accept yourself, and enjoy the journey of creating yourself from moment to moment.

Lesson #15:

Base your self-worth on your character, not on what you own, how much education you have, or your physical appearance.

Exercise:

Evaluate what criteria you have been using to value yourself. Begin to realize that true self-worth comes from self-acceptance, being true to yourself, and taking full responsibility for who you are. Look into a mirror, and repeat these affirmations as often as necessary to realign your definition of self-worth.

"I am beautiful, compassionate, and perfect just the way I am."

"I am worthy of my love and the love of others."

"I love the person I am and who I am becoming."

~ 16 ~

Set Boundaries

"People are like dirt. They can either nourish you and help you grow as a person, or they can stunt your growth and make you wilt and die." ~ *Plato*

Do you have trouble setting boundaries? In any relationship (whether it is with family, spouse, or friends), it is our responsibility to set the boundaries of how we allow others to treat us. It is not their fault if we allow them to use us, verbally abuse us, or take without ever giving back. Loving people does not mean you need to let them use you. If there are people in your life that you feel are using you, you need to reset the boundaries. Learn to say, "No." People only treat us as bad as we allow.

You can love someone without letting him or her in the inner circle of your life. The inner circle should be reserved for those who love and support you. Your time, attention, and companionship are gifts. They are the gift of presence. You have the power and the right to decide who shares your presence. You can't change people and their patterns of social interactions, but you can change your patterns of social interactions. All it takes is enough awareness to see the part you play in the relationship. With awareness comes choice. Awareness gives you the ability to choose to set appropriate boundaries, so you won't feel used.

Lesson #16:

It is your responsibility to set the boundaries of how you allow other people to treat you.

Exercise:

Do you feel like someone is using you? Evaluate the situation to see if you have been allowing this behavior. Do you need to establish boundaries or reset current boundaries? Realize that if you have agreed to certain behavior, then no one is using you. Your time and attention are yours to decide who you give them to. You are not being used unless you have agreed to be used.

Work on establishing appropriate boundaries in your relationships. Begin watching how you interact with others, to raise your awareness of the part you play in how others treat you. The more you pay attention to your own patterns of social interaction, the more you will start to see where the boundaries are in the relationship. If they need adjusting, you have the responsibility to yourself to clearly communicate that you only interact with people who respect your personal boundaries.

Take Responsibility for Your Life

I am now whom I choose to be,
Consciously guiding my destiny.
I once blamed fate for losing my way,
But, actions past formed me today.
I was asleep—slumbering life;
Dreaming daily; Seeding strife.
Now, I pick, plan persist,
Intending to be whom I insist.
Dueling demons; Fighting fear,
Actions my weapons; Thoughts my seer.
I will endure until the end,
Minding each moment that I spend,
Knowing that I'm forever free,
Being now whom I choose to be.

"Choose to Be" from Awakening Perception

When we blame other people for our problems and personal issues, we become puppets of life. To be completely free and at peace with yourself and the world, you have to stop pointing the finger away from yourself for being who you are and for the way you act.

Unhappy people tend to blame their parents, bosses, past traumas, ex-spouses, or even God for their problems. They prefer to play the victim with *Woe is me* stories rather than looking at their own actions and life choices. Unhappy people say things like, "I'm this way because of _____." They place the responsibility of why they are the way they are on other people and situations instead of taking the responsibility themselves. By acting like a puppet of life, they release any responsibility of why they act the way they do and believe that they have no control in who they are. As long as they play the part of the puppet, they are right: They have no control and very little personal power.

To be truly happy, you must take charge of life by accepting that who and what you are today is a direct result of all of the thoughts and actions that you have made in the past, not because of someone else or something outside yourself. People have the power to choose to be any way they wish to be. Don't be a victim of life! Once one accepts responsibility for one's own life, true change occurs.

When I realized that I alone was responsible for how I interact with others and respond to life events, it gave me the power to make different choices. I was no longer a victim of life. I began to choose to look deeper into myself and to take a hard look at how I interacted in the world. I discovered my habits based in fear were not working to create the life I desired. I learned to face my fears and to focus on love, joy, and life's beauty. In doing so, I chose to be a happy free spirit. Reclaim your personal power by taking full responsibility for who you are and how you interact with the world. Take responsibility for your life. Cut those puppet strings!

Lesson #17:

You are responsible for your interactions with people and your responses to situations in life.

Exercise:

Do you blame others or past situations for your unhappiness? When you blame others, it takes the responsibility and control of life away from you. Take your life back. You have full control over who you are and how you choose to be now and in the future. Stop being a victim and take responsibility for yourself. Regain control of the wheel and start steering your life in the direction you choose. Take time to really contemplate how much blame versus self-responsibility you practice in your life. Be honest with yourself. If you find an issue where you still feel like a victim, repeat the following affirmations:

"I am fully responsible for how I interact with others."

"I am fully responsible for my responses to life situations."

"I am fully responsible for who I choose to be."

~ 18 ~

Be Grateful

"Celebrate. Celebration is an expression of Gratitude.
Gratitude is like the prayer, while Celebration is
the hymn and sacred dance. Celebration is a road to happiness."
- Jonathan Lockwood Huie

Now that you have planted the seeds of acceptance and have weeded out most of the complaints in your life, it's time to plant more seeds of happiness. The attitude of gratitude is one of those seeds.

One of the best ways to deal with life's trials is to maintain an attitude of gratitude. By being grateful for what you have, it takes the focus off what you wish were different. When you are in a state of gratitude, you are focusing on the positive. There are so many things in life that we take for granted. When you take time to focus on these, you are generating feelings of happiness. Be grateful for the life that you have right now. Don't get caught up in waiting for a better life tomorrow.

Ponder this quote by Frances Rodman: "Just think how happy you would be if you lost everything you have right now, and then got it back again."

This profound statement makes you appreciate your life right now, as it is. Many people will go through life with the attitude of the cup being half empty. They tend to focus on what is lacking in life, never really appreciating what they have now. Others see the cup as half full. They spend life focusing on what they have and do not emphasize what seems to be missing. This is a more positive attitude than viewing the cup half empty. Many of you are familiar with this cup half empty/ half full analogy. But there is a third option, which the great Buddhist teacher Ajahn Chah would encourage his students to contemplate. He would hold up his cup of tea and say that he appreciates the way the sunlight reflects off the glass and the way the cup feels in his hand. He would appreciate the cup in its entirety, full, half full, or empty, for he knows that in time the cup will someday be broken. In this world, everything in life is temporary. Nothing lasts forever. Everything has a limited existence. We are born and every day we are one step closer to our death. All relationships will have an end; all things will eventually be broken. Every aspect of life is as impermanent as spring flowers. Knowing this, we must embrace every minute of every relationship with appreciation and every day with gratitude for life itself.

It is easy to forget to be grateful. There are so many relationships and luxuries that become so commonplace that you take it for granted that they will always be there. You begin to think that these things are entitled to you. You never really consider what life would be without them. If you have the good fortune to have eaten today or even yesterday, have indoor plumbing or electricity, then you are living like a king compared to many people in the world. Be grateful for the luxuries that have become commonplace in your life. Take a moment to really ponder the fortunate life that you live. Most of the problems you might think you have are just minor inconveniences compared to the real problems in the world. Be grateful that your biggest issue today was your air-conditioning breaking, your car breaking down, or having a headache. It could be so much worse.

When you have an attitude of gratitude in your life, you will count your blessings when things seem to go wrong. You will be thankful that you didn't hurt someone when the tire blew on your car. When something unexpected happens, you will be thankful that you learned how to respond with conscious action instead of react to life with irritation. You will be thankful that you have the opportunity to sit with your family or friends at dinner and you will be thankful for the food. The attitude of gratitude will give you a positive way of viewing the world with appreciation.

Be grateful for the loved ones in your life. These are the people who are usually taken for granted the most. Take time to acknowledge them, and tell them how grateful you are for their presence in your life. Tell them that they make a difference. Show them your appreciation. Don't wait, because tomorrow could be too late. Remember, the cup is already broken.

Lesson #18:

The attitude of gratitude will increase your happiness.

Exercise:

Be grateful. Understand that the cup is already broken.

When things seem to go wrong, remind yourself that they could be worse. Be grateful that they are not. Focus on the blessings of life, not the obstacles.

Begin to practice gratitude as often as possible. Count your blessings. You might want to start each day with an affirmation of gratitude of your choosing.

"I'm so thankful for this day. Life is a gift."

"I thank God for this day I'm about to live."

Also, you may want to start taking a few seconds to be thankful for your daily meals before you eat them. Bring the attitude of gratitude into your life in any way you choose, and you will be thankful that you did!

~ 19 ~

Everyone Has His or Her Own Garden

So far we have learned that life is like a flower garden and we are the ones who plant the seeds. We either unconsciously let the garden get overrun with weeds of dissatisfaction or we can consciously take control of our garden, planting beautiful flowers of happiness. We've practiced changing the way we respond to life and gained awareness of how our thoughts and attention can be used as a tool for creating a life of joy and peace.

The next step involves exploring the concept that everyone has his or her own separate flower garden. Each garden is as personal as the person who tends it. Not everyone's garden will be a floral work of art. As a matter of fact, most people's gardens are filled with weeds of unhappiness choking the life out of a few happy moments in their lives.

One of the most challenging aspects of owning a garden is keeping out the weeds. When people who have neglected their garden interact with others, they spread their weeds. This is not intentional. This is never personal. They are not trying to ruin your happy state of being. They aren't even aware that they have a garden or that they should pay attention to it. They believe that life is filled with unhappy events, that some days are good and some days are bad, and that they have no control over any of it. They have learned to focus on the unhappy events and to share them repeatedly throughout the day.

You can't change people. Their weeds have been building up over a lifetime and actually the only one who is capable of weeding is the one who owns the garden. Even though you can't change people, you can change how you respond to them. When someone is taking their frustrations out on you, instead of reacting, being upset yourself, you can choose to act with awareness. Remember your ABCs: Awareness, Breathe, Choose a response. Your response may be to just ignore the comment. It might be to respond in a positive way, or it might be just telling them you don't want to hear about it. Take a moment to have compassion on them, because they are filled with unhappiness in that moment. See them for what they are: unhappy people just letting off steam. Above all, remember it is never personal. It's not about you; it's about *their* state of being.

When people say negative things to you, you can make sure the weeds don't take root in your garden. To do this, you have to realize that what people say and do is a result of their own state mind at the time. It actually doesn't have anything to do with you. It's never personal. When people complain about life, they are just expressing their unhappy thoughts that have built up. The unhappy thoughts germinate into unhappy moods. All the negative thoughts create negative energy that needs to be discharged.

If you realize that what they are saying isn't personal but is just a result of their mind filled with unhappy weeds, then you will see that what they say has nothing to do with you. It is no more personal than if your neighbor's dandelion seeds spread onto your lawn at home.

It is very important not to let those weeds germinate in your garden. You won't be able to keep the weeds from spreading in your garden if you allow them to take seed. The first step is to be aware when the weeds are blowing your way. Once you notice them, you will be able to change the flow of the wind so that they just fly past your garden.

So what are these weeds that people blow our way every day? It's all the negative things people say to you and negative emotions thrown at you. It's listening to complaints. It's when your spouse snaps at you because he can't find his keys. It's your boss yelling at you because she's in a bad mood. It's the person who just cut you off in traffic and then beeped at you like it was your fault. It's your teenager when he doesn't want to talk to you because, well, he is a moody teen. It's all the negatively charged emotions and words that you encounter all day.

Lesson #19:

Everyone has his or her own garden. Some are full of the weeds of stress and unhappiness. Don't let other people's weeds take root in your garden!

Exercise:

Begin to bring your attention to your interactions with people. If they try to spread their unhappiness with you, respond with awareness instead of reacting. Take a breath, and bring your full attention on remaining calm. When you see the weeds blowing your way, see them for what they are. Remind yourself that it isn't personal. They are just expressing their unhappiness. Keep your focus on having compassion for them, because they are suffering from their own bad moods. Let those weeds fly right by your beautiful flower garden, and go about your day as if they never happened.

If you find yourself becoming upset and repeating the negative interaction over and over in your mind, then the weed has taken root. It's not too late. When you notice that your mind is dwelling on negative thoughts, the sooner you stop it the easier it will be to uproot. Gently bring your attention back to the present moment. Take a deep breath and pay attention to where you are now, what you are doing now. Bring your full attention to whatever you are doing in the moment. Each time the negative train of thought comes to mind, don't pay attention to it. Let it flow right through. Do not jump on any train of thought that will bring you to an unhappy destination. The more you practice this, the easier it will be to let the thoughts flow without getting your attention hooked. Again, don't judge your efforts. It took a lifetime to build the habit of jumping on every train of thought without question. It will take some time to break the habit.

Every tiny bit of awareness that you bring to this endeavor will pay off.

~ 20 ~

The Mule in the Well

There once was an old mule that fell into an old dry well. When he realized he was stuck in the well, he brayed and brayed until the farmer heard his cries. The farmer looked down at the old mule in the well and knew it would be impossible to lift him out. He thought about the situation and decided that since the mule and the well were old and useless, he should fill in the well, burying the mule to put him out of his misery. So the farmer began to shovel dirt into the well on top of the mule. Then something surprising happened! As each pile of dirt came down on the mule, he would shake it off and climb on top of it. Eventually, he was high enough to jump out of the well. (Retelling of story; author unknown.)

When I first heard this story, I realized that I am like the old mule. Some people may think I am useless and don't have much life in me, but that's not how I see myself. Like the mule, I rise above what others think of me, shake off whatever dirt comes my way, and always look for the deeper meaning and lesson that I can learn from a situation or event. With this perspective on challenging situations, I am able to raise my awareness and understanding of life and myself.

When life seems to throw dirt your way, trying to bury you or keep you down, shake it off and rise above it! This is when you realize that even what seems to be a problem or a tragic circumstance can be used as a lesson to move you to a higher level of awareness.

Lesson #20:

What seems like a tragic circumstance can be used as a lesson to move you to a higher level of awareness.

Exercise:

    Do you feel stuck without a way out of a situation that is beyond your control? Perhaps by shaking the situation off your mind you can rise above it. It may be something that you can't do much about externally, but by shrugging it off you will be releasing yourself in the process. Problems are nothing more than a train of thought in your mind. Don't dwell on them, and they reduce in size.

~ 21 ~

Worrying Is a Seed of Suffering

"He who fears he shall suffer, already suffers what he fears." ~ *Michel de Montaigne*

Be aware of your fears, face them with courage, for it is not what you are afraid of that will destroy you, it is the fear itself that has that power. It isn't always the big fears that destroy your peace of mind. It is usually the little fears called *worries* that bring suffering.

When a worry comes into your mind, recognize it for what it is: *fear*. Do not allow fear to rule you. There is never a need to worry, because worrying does not change the outcome of an event. It is wasted mental energy that will cause suffering. Worrying destroys peace of mind and happiness. Any time that we allow ourselves to indulge in worrying, we have given into fear. Remember lesson #6: What you focus on affects your level of happiness or misery.

Worrying and being prepared for the future are two separate thought processes. Being in the mind-set of *what could go wrong* can work to your advantage if you allow it to push you to be prepared with a plan B or to take proactive steps to ensure undesired outcomes are averted. In contrast, excessive worrying about things you have no control over will disturb your peace of mind.

Learn to distinguish between these two types thinking. If you can take action to prevent an undesirable outcome, then be proactive by planning as you deem necessary. Then let the thoughts go by reminding yourself that you have done what you can do and are prepared for whatever the future unfolds. If you have no control over what you may imagine happening, then there is no need to waste your mental energy upsetting yourself. Use whatever methods you find work for you to jump off the worry train of thought. Just by being aware that you are caught up in worrying is one step closer to stopping it.

Lesson #21:

Worrying is a waste of mental energy and destroys peace of mind.

Exercise:

Begin to be aware of when your mind wanders onto worries. When you are worrying, take appropriate action if possible to alleviate the worry. If the situation you are worried about is out of your control, then jump off the worry train of thought. Take a slow, deep breath and refocus your mind on being present or on more uplifting trains of thought. The more you practice not worrying, the less apt you will be to focus on things out of your control. All thoughts feed on attention. Don't feed worries and they go away.

Worrying is a major form of mental suffering for some people. If your mind tends to worry, becoming aware of it is the first step to retraining yourself not to worry. Any amount of practice you spend on being aware of what you are thinking and jumping off undesirable trains of thought will pay off. Don't judge your efforts. You are on your way to being free of the little fears called worries.

~ 22 ~

Circling Trains of Thought

" **I** can't stop thinking about _____ and it's upsetting me." We have all been there at one time. It may be a past pain or a future worry that is disturbing your peace of mind. You may have tried to be present to keep the thought at bay, but it just keeps coming back, circling in your mind over and over. Here are a few hyper-focus techniques that will effectively block those haunting thoughts:

Create: When you focus on a new garden project, cooking a new recipe, or redecorating a room, you are paying attention to the process of creation. Creative thought is a right-brain activity, while negative trains of thought, such as worries and dwelling on the past, are left-brain activities. Engaging in creative thought will switch your brain to the more relaxing right-brain perception, which is generally focused on whatever you are doing in the moment. My favorite creative endeavors are cooking soup, making sandcastles, and coloring.

Play games: Playing games will focus your attention enough to stop all other thoughts from taking over your mind. If you are alone, try puzzles, word games, or Sudoku. Scrabble is my favorite. Playing board games has the added value of nurturing relationships. (I highly recommend this to all families.) Playing sports has the added benefit of exercise. Even watching sports can sometimes be enough to grab your attention and keep your focus outside your head.

Music: Singing happy songs will hyper-focus your mind on breathing, tone, rhythm, etc. Karaoke requires even more attention by having to read at the same time. This will effectively keep your mind from wandering onto negative trains of thought. You also get the bonus of deep breathing. Playing a musical instrument also requires your full attention. These activities are like musical meditation!

Service: When we are helping others, we are focused away from our own problems. Volunteer in your community or church. When you are of service, you are not only being a productive member of your community, but you will feel better about yourself.

Dance: Get up and dance for a few minutes. Dance to a routine, or make up the moves as you go. Any kind of dancing will do the trick! Make dancing a regular part of your life for physical as well as mental health.

Of course, keep practicing breathing and being present as much as possible, but sometimes these techniques may be just what you need to break the negative train of thought and force you into the now.

Lesson #22:

Being hyper-focused on an activity can effectively stop negative trains of thought from circling in your mind.

Exercise:

Become aware if you get caught up in unhappy thoughts that keep circling in your mind. When you find that a few deep breaths are not enough to jump off the train of thought, then use a hyper-focus technique to keep those disturbing thoughts at bay. You will discover which types of techniques work best for you. Enjoy practicing these working meditation techniques, or discover your own ways hyper-focusing your mind.

~ 23 ~

Make Peace with the Past

Dream of what will be,
but accept what may come.
Be grateful for what was,
and let what's done be done.
~LB Shannon

Making peace with your past is an important step in achieving peace of mind and happiness. The first step is to stop rehashing the stories that cause you suffering. By repeating these stories, you reinforce the negative emotions. It is time to eliminate the habit of focusing on past emotional baggage. This is accomplished by becoming aware of when you are thinking about such issues, then immediately jumping off that train of thought. One of the easiest techniques for jumping off negative trains of thought is to bring your awareness back to the present moment by focusing on your five senses. Get outside your head and become fully present. Pay attention to life as it is happening instead of living life in your head and thinking about the past. The more you practice, the less the thoughts will come, and the easier it will be to let go of your pain.

Some people feel such overwhelming emotional pain that they don't know how they could ever get past it. Emotional pain is like fire. When you direct attention its way, it gets an emotional surge and the flames get bigger and hotter. The first step is to stop focusing on the pain and stop repeating the story over and over to your friends and to yourself in your mind.

The second step is to make peace with the past. In order to make peace with your past, you must begin to realize that when people do and say things to hurt other people it is a reflection of their own fears and emotional pain. As you move toward happiness and peace of mind, you will begin to have compassion on them because they are stuck in darkness and are suffering. Ponder this thought:

> *"If we could read the secret history of our enemies,*
> *we should find in each man's life sorrow and*
> *suffering enough to disarm all hostility."*
> *~ Henry Wadsworth Longfellow*

Whatever people do is never about you; it is about them and their state of mind at the time. They are reacting to their own emotional suffering. Reflect on these thoughts when you feel anger and resentment toward another. This will help you move past the emotional pain and finally let it go.

Keep in mind that every experience in life has a lesson, even tragic experiences. If we suffer through something without learning in the process, then that would be a real tragedy.

Lesson #23:

Emotional pain is like fire. When you direct attention its way, it fuels the fire.

Exercise:

Are you holding onto an emotional pain that you feel you will never get over? Set the intent right now to believe that you will be able to get past this and to get to a point of compassion and peace with the situation. Repeat this affirmation: "I will learn to live with this without feeling hurt."

Do not feed the emotional fire with your attention. Jump off trains of thought that are leading to this issue. When you aren't as focused on the pain, it will subside a bit. This will give you enough personal power to begin to heal the issue in your heart.

When you feel ready to begin healing, start this simple one-minute meditation: Imagine the person who is involved with your issue. Imagine him standing right in front of you. Say to yourself, "Peace be with you." Then offer him your compassion by imagining embracing him so that both of you are healed. Imagine the *feeling* more than the visualization. It is through our feelings that we heal. If this exercise is too much, then go back to it another time. Deep emotional pain can take time to heal. Be patient with yourself as you practice moving into a more present and happy state of being.

~ 24 ~

Reconnect with Your Inner Child

"Too many people grow up. That's the trouble with the world,
too many people grow up. They forget. They don't remember
what it's like to be twelve years old." ~ Walt Disney

When we were children, we were free. We lived in the moment, focusing on just being a child. If you are over forty, like me, then you were probably never bored when you were young. This seems to be a new phenomenon among our youth in the last twenty years or so. No, when I was young I was never bored. I played outside with or without toys, with or without friends. Whatever I was doing was all that mattered at the time.

As we got older, we lost that feeling of freedom to live in the moment. We became slaves to our wondering minds, often thinking about the past or the future and not really living in the moment. We become absent in our own lives. The body breathes, walks, and performs actions, but the mind is somewhere else. When we consciously bring our attention to the present moment, we become like little children again. We enjoy our life with more vigor. We begin to be present in our own life.

When you are free like a child, you naturally express your innate creativity and wonder. Children use their imaginations, opening their world to endless possibilities. They are naturally inquisitive, creative, playful, and willing to explore their worlds. When they create, they create for the joy of expressing themselves. They have an innate understanding that the act of creating is the what is important, not the end result. They do not dwell on the imperfections of their artistic

66

expression, nor are they attached to the end result. They just create for the sake of creating. Thus, they build their sand castles with joy, not worrying that they are only temporary. They live in the moment, being fully present. It is time to live like a child again.

When you become present, you will pay more attention to your surroundings. You will notice the flowers as you walk into the bank; you will notice the stars at night and maybe take time to watch the sunset. You will have more time to pursue creative activities and more time to play. How can you have more time? Remember how long summer vacations used to seem when you were young? The more present you are, the slower time seems to flow. Just try watching and waiting for a teapot to boil, and you will experience how time slows down when you are present. When you aren't stuck inside your head and are actually present, time seems to expand.

Practice being present and you will begin to awaken the little child inside you. Everything will become more fun. Your inner child will want to play because children love to play. They enjoy being outside in nature, looking at clouds, even playing in the rain! Your inner child might want to try new things, play games, redecorate a room, or make the food on the dinner plate look pretty. Be present and you will feel an urge to express new wonder, playfulness, and creativity.

Lesson #24:

Reconnecting with your inner child makes life fun, full of wonder and expands time.

Exercise:

Practice bringing childlike awareness into something that you normally do without awareness. It could be as simple as taking a walk. If you normally are caught up in thoughts while walking, switch your awareness to your surroundings. Take a new route. Make a game out of it. How many animals can you see along the way? How many distinct sounds are around you? Does one street smell different from another street? If you were blindfolded, would you be able to know which street you were on?

Or maybe awaken your inner child while making dinner. Instead of being caught up in thoughts about the past or future, pay attention to what you are cooking. Make a new recipe, or use your creativity in presentation and table-setting design. Feel the textures of the different foods as you prepare them. Take a moment to smell them, delighting in the variety of scents. Be present, and the experience will be totally different from mindlessly making dinner while listening to TV.

Practice reconnecting with your inner child, and life will be filled with playful wonder!

~ 25 ~

Letting Go of Anger

*"Throughout life people will make you mad, disrespect you,
and treat you bad. Let God deal with the things they do cause
hate in your heart will consume you too." ~Will Smith*

A fundamental step to being happy is learning to process negative emotions in a healthy way. When we are born, we freely express our emotions with passion, letting them completely flow. As children we processed emotions with full force: we cried hard and laughed out loud. Then we moved on with our day, not thinking about it any more. Children let their emotions flow with complete passion and then release them. They can be angry one minute and laughing the next. As we got older, we learned to suppress our emotions and/or express them in unhealthy ways. We also learned to dwell on the emotions in our thoughts, keeping them stuck inside our emotional bodies.

When we allow our thoughts to dwell in anger, discontent, or injustice, we are causing our own suffering. Anger, as all emotions, is a natural response to some situations. We must relearn how to feel the emotion, let it flow and let it go. We all did this when we were very young. We would get upset, cry, scream, and jump up and down, and then a few minutes later we would be onto something else without dwelling on the past.

When people stay with the emotion by repetitively rehashing the situation in their minds, suffering occurs. Anger itself is the demon that wields the punishment. If we could instantly feel the burning nature of anger like the burn of a fire, we would avoid touching it again. There are many ways to extinguish this emotional fire. The one that works best for me is taking a few slow, deep breaths. This is instantly calming and allows your attention to move away from the angry thoughts. The fire of anger feeds on attention. Don't feed it, and it won't burn you.

Anger is never an excuse to act in harmful ways toward others. We all feel angry from time to time. With any negative emotion, it is best to let it flow to let it go. But that doesn't mean you have to yell at someone or resort to violence. When you feel angry, acknowledge it, take a few slow, deep breaths, and then, if the feeling is still strong, choose an appropriate way to channel it: Walk, run, jump, scream (never at someone), take a shower, exercise, sing, or cry. Use whatever method works for you to discharge the emotion without spreading it to others.

Lesson #25:

Let emotions flow, then let them go.

Exercise:

Begin processing your negative emotions in healthy ways. Practice using different techniques to calm yourself and to release the emotional energy. Discover what methods work best for you. *Be aware of your responsibility to keep your negative emotions from attacking others either verbally or physically.*

~ 26 ~

Connect with Nature

The ocean is my sanctuary,
Where I return like rivers and rain,
Reminding me of the greater whole,
from whence my soul once came.

"Ocean" from *Awakening Perception*

As I lay in the hammock in my backyard, a big yellow butterfly passes by, capturing my attention. I am immediately transported to a world of floral delight, fluttering from flower to flower. I feel the wind blow and begin losing myself in the movement of the leaves mixed with the shadows in the tree above me. After a few minutes, I gaze through an opening in the tree canopy, focusing on the passing clouds; each animated shape becomes alive before it dissolves into the blue background. A mocking bird calls me back to earth, and then the melodic sound of the waterfall entrances me with its gentle rumble.

Take time to be with nature, time to be one with nature. The above backyard meditation is easy to do. Just sit quietly and observe your surroundings *without commentary*. Use your senses and explore the wonders of the natural world.

No matter how far mankind has tried to distance himself from nature, the fact remains that humans are a part of nature. We live in a time where people have learned to spend most of their day disconnected from Mother Nature. We spend time in a variety of boxes that separate us from our natural surroundings. There is the house where you live, perhaps spending half your day or more inside this domestic box. There may be the building where you work, and some of you even have a little office or a cubicle box. There are the mobile boxes, such as cars, buses, and trains. We spend our time moving from one box to another, keeping ourselves as far away from nature as possible.

Watching nature is viewed from television sets and computers. The art of sitting outside, relaxing, and just being with nature is becoming uncommon. The electronic age has taken over our minds, luring us to spend countless hours watching TV, connected to the Internet, hooked up to our headphones, and glued to our cell phones waiting for the next text message or tweet. Our minds are being hooked by audiovisual electronic stimuli to the point where we have tuned out what we feel with our body and the smell and taste of our food because we aren't paying attention. We are forgetting that the purpose of having a physical body is so that we can experience the world through our senses.

Not all of you are disconnected from nature, but most unhappy people have this in common. If you are one of those people, get out of your box! By getting fresh air and sunshine, you will give yourself a boost of happiness. Take a short walk, read outside, go for a hike, go fishing, go camping, bike, or just sit quietly outside taking in the sights and sounds. You will begin to reconnect with the natural world. You'll begin to notice your habitat and surroundings. You'll become aware of and even stop to watch birds and butterflies. The more you can incorporate being outside in nature, the bigger the emotional reward will be.

Besides the relaxing benefits of reconnecting with nature, the human body benefits from sunlight itself. The amount of sunlight we receive affects our levels of vitamin D. Vitamin D is absorbed through exposure to sunlight. Studies have shown that low levels of vitamin D may cause some people to feel symptoms of depression. So sunshine can actually brighten your day emotionally! Take a few minutes every day to bask in the sunlight and renew your spirit.

When we take time to connect with nature, we recharge our spirits and relax our minds. Being outside encourages us to use our senses as they were meant to be used: experiencing our surroundings. We give ourselves the opportunity to feel the sunlight, rain, and wind. We can experience the sweet sound of bird songs and be a witness the miracle of flight. We can ground ourselves by digging our toes in the sand or smelling the freshness of damp grass on a summer morning. Being with nature allows us to be present, which reduces stress and rejuvenates the soul. Our world is alive. We are animals of the natural world, not apart from but a part of nature. When we reconnect, we come home again. Increase your awareness of your surroundings, and you may be surprised how much it enhances your life.

Lesson #26:

Being with nature encourages presence, which reduces stress and rejuvenates the soul.

Exercise:

Spend some time every day outside. Incorporate outdoor activities as much as possible. Practice being with nature. Learn to hear the sounds, distinguish the scents, and appreciate the sights of the natural world. If you find thoughts of the past or the future coming to mind, refocus on your surroundings. This exercise helps train your ability to focus and to be present while rejuvenating yourself at the same time.

Suggestions:

- Sit quietly, close your eyes, and listen to as many distinct sounds as you can sense. The world is alive with sound. The wind blows, the birds sing, squirrels chatter, and bees buzz. How many sounds can you sense?

- Lie or sit under a tree and feel the cool grass or earth beneath you. Imagine the intricate root system of life beneath you. You are lying within the life energy of the tree. Feel the energy. Watch the movement and pay attention to the shadows of the leaves as they move. The tree is alive. Connect with this living system of energy.

- Close your eyes and see how many distinct scents you can detect. Everything emits a scent. Can you distinguish between a clover and a blade of grass? Can you smell the freshness after a rain or the stillness after a snow?

- Sky watch. Gaze at the clouds or the stars. Lose yourself in the shapes of the clouds as they dance across the sky. Watch a moon-rise. Lose yourself in the moon shadows.

- Sit outside by an open fire. Watch the way the flames dance, becoming an animated system of energy. Listen to the crackling and popping. Enjoy the smoky aroma of the different types of wood. Feel the heat on your body, on your hands and bottoms of your feet. Watch the smoke as it rises, as it dances its way upward. Notice the way the logs burn, turning into a world of glowing coals. (This is one of my favorite outside activities.)

~ 27 ~

Two Men Go to the Park

Mr. Chipper and Mr. Grim go to the park for their morning walk. Mr. Chipper sees a few mourning doves foraging for their daily feast. He throws them some breadcrumbs. Mr. Grim says, "Oh, why did you have to do that? Now they are going to bother us for more. All they do is poop on every park bench as it is!" Mr. Chipper ignores him and a few minutes later stops to smell the newly bloomed daisies along the side of the path. Mr. Grim sarcastically says, "Great! The flowers are in bloom! Soon there will be pollen all over everything. I'll have to take an allergy pill as soon as I get home." Mr. Chipper ignores him as they stop to sit on a park bench for a while. Mr. Chipper enjoys feeling the morning sun on his face and the cool wind blowing through his hair. He loves to sit with nature and just be still. Mr. Grim says, "Oh, look at all these cigarette butts! People are no darn good, I tell you! They have no consideration!" Mr. Chipper gets up and picks up the three cigarette butts that are right near Mr. Grimm's feet. He gently tosses them and a stray candy wrapper into the garbage pail next to the bench. He then sits down to enjoy the sun and gentle wind again. After a minute, Mr. Grim says, "Come on, let's get out of here. The sun is no good for my skin, and the wind is messing up my hair." Mr. Chipper gets up and joyfully walks his friend home.

Both men were in the same place at the same time but had two very different experiences. Happiness isn't caused by your external environment. It is the way you process the environment. You can either focus your attention on all the beauty, and what is pleasant, or you can focus your attention on everything that seems to be wrong with the world. The world is the same; it's the way you look at it that will make life either happy or miserable for yourself.

Mr. Grim couldn't enjoy the walk because he wasn't really on the walk. He was caught up inside his head with negative trains of thought. Mr. Chipper stayed present, allowing himself to experience the beauty of nature. When he became aware of the cigarette butts, he took action to remove them instead of complaining about them and doing nothing about it. Mr. Chipper has also learned that to respond to Mr. Grimm's unhappy statements only encourages him to complain more and keeps himself from enjoying the walk.

Lesson #27:

The more you become aware of how you perceive the world, the more power you will have to change your perception to one more positive.

Exercise:

Ask yourself if you are more like Mr. Chipper or Mr. Grim. See if you can catch yourself when you act like Mr. Grim. If you find yourself in a *Grim moment,* take a deep breath and realign your attention on a more Chipper perspective.

The way you look at the world will either make life happy or miserable for yourself.

~ 28 ~

Exercise Helps Elevate Moods

Our physical bodies have an effect on our emotional bodies. If we are physically out of shape, it can have an enormous effect on how we feel emotionally. When we take steps to stay physically healthy and fit, we are increasing our emotional health as well.

Exercise doesn't have to be difficult or vigorous to affect your emotional body. Exercising, even with just a short walk, will increase your oxygen intake, relieve stress, and elevate your mood. Walking is one of the best and easiest activities to relieve stress.

Make walking a daily habit. Even if you only walk for fifteen minutes, it will make a difference in the way you feel both physically and emotionally. Walk outside when possible and gain the added benefits of fresh air and sunshine. Take a friend or family member for a walk and you'll have quality bonding time.

As you walk, pay attention to all the sights, sounds, and smells. This brings your awareness to the present, which makes it a walking meditation. Make walking a daily habit and you will be exercising your body and easing your mind at the same time. Walk more and enjoy life more.

I cannot over emphasize the importance of exercise for those of you who are prone to depression or are bi-polar. Whenever I feel the downward pull of my cycle towards depression, if I force myself to keep walking daily, it really helps to keep me from spiraling further into depression. Walking is one of my most important tools for maintaining stability and balance during emotional swings.

Lesson #28:

Exercise helps elevate moods.

Exercise:

Incorporate some form of exercise into your life. At the very least, make walking a daily habit. If you start exercising every day, you will reap the benefits both physically and mentally.

~ 29 ~

To Each His Own Journey

A young man in search of wisdom asked, "Please tell me, Grandmother, how can I attain wisdom such as yours? Which path should I take to follow you?"

The wise old Grandmother replied, "Dear child, you can journey to where I am, but you cannot follow me. The path to wisdom is a personal journey. There are many different roads to take and no two are ever the same. You will find many guides and signs leading you along the path to wisdom, but only you can make the choices at each fork in the road."

"But, Grandmother, how will I know which way to go when I reach a fork in the road?"

"Dear child, do not fret over which road to choose. All paths eventually lead to the same place. Some may look easier and faster if you are following in someone else's path, but it is when you make your own way, following your own path, that you will not only get where you are going, but you'll have found yourself in the process."

Resist the urge to think that your way or your path is the right way or only way. Allow others to travel their life journeys according to their own hearts. By respecting the beliefs and choices of others, we have no need to defend our own. It demonstrates that we acknowledge that everyone has his or her own path to forge, including ourselves. When we try to control other people, we are taking away their personal power, and diminishing their free will.

Allowing others to walk their own path does not mean we have to indulge people caught up in victim mentality. Those are the people who seem to be looking for advice but actually just want to draw you into their drama. They are looking for sympathy, not solutions. Years ago, I used to give advice to others and when they didn't follow my direction it would cause me to feel frustrated. I was attached to the outcome of how I thought they should act. If we can get to a place where we can offer guidance without attachment, have compassion for those who are still struggling to find themselves, and have a let-go-and-let-God attitude, then we release ourselves from stressing over other people's lives.

Conversely, when we constantly seek guidance and approval of our choices, we give our personal power away. Seek wise advice as necessary, but always make the choice according to your own heart. Decide if what you are choosing is aligned with who you are. Is it aligned with your values and dreams of the future? Is the choice made out of love or out of fear? These questions will help you evaluate your life decisions. In the end, there really is no wrong choice made with awareness and love.

You may decide that after a time you want to make a new choice in another direction. That is fine too, because all paths are tools for self-introspection and offer lessons in life. Never regret anything in the past if you have learned an important lesson through the experience. Forgive yourself for being human. We all make choices that in hindsight we would do differently. Yet we all do the best we can with the level of awareness we have at the time. Maya Angelou says it well: "When you know better, you do better." Also, if you are tolerant of your mistakes, then you'll be tolerant when others make the same mistakes.

Lesson #29:

Life is a personal journey of self-discovery. Allow others to have a chance to find themselves in their own way.

Exercise:

Does it upset you when people close to you don't follow your advice? Practice bringing awareness into the situation. Release your need to control their life choices because you know what is best for them. What is best for them is to figure out what is best for themselves by learning to follow their authentic self. Practice guidance without expectation. Be supportive of your loved ones even when they make choices that are different from what you would do.

Do you constantly seek approval or guidance from others? Seek wise advice as necessary, but always make the choice according to your own heart.

Ask yourself these questions when you need to make a decision:
Is what you are choosing aligned with who you are?
Is it aligned with your values and dreams of the future?
Is the choice made out of love or out of fear?
These questions will help you evaluate your life decisions. In the end, there really is no wrong choice made with awareness and love.

~ 30 ~

Releasing Regret

"If only. Those must be the two saddest words in the world." ~ Mercedes Lackey

"Never regret. If it's good it's wonderful. If it's bad it's experience." ~ Victoria Holt

When we hold onto regrets, it hinders our ability to fully enjoy life. It creates a darkness that clouds our inner joy. To truly enjoy life, we need to make peace with our past by accepting it for what it was. You must release any thoughts about how the past should have been any different from it was. These types of thoughts are pointless and they only serve to disturb your peace of mind. Come to accept that whatever happened is over now. To think about how you wish it had been different is riding on a train of thought that leads to emotional suffering. Don't be attached to imaginary past scenarios by rewriting history in your mind. Use your imagination to focus on future dreams, not to torture yourself with thoughts of what should have been or what could have been different.

For some people, thinking about what could have been is the root of personal regret. You may look back and ponder different choices you might have made that would have resulted in different events occurring. As tempting as this mind candy can be, we must be aware of how destructive this way of thinking is to our peace of mind. The *if only* scenarios reinforce the negative emotions about what actually happened. It won't help you get past the regret; it will ignite it with each thought of *If I had only done this.* If you feel regret about something you did or see now that you should have done something different, that means that you have come to a higher awareness of yourself and life.

This is an important lesson. Now that you know better, you will choose to act differently in the future. Do not regret your past actions. They are lessons you learned the hard way. Share your experience with others so that they may learn not to make similar mistakes. Listen to others to learn lessons from their experiences.

Be aware that you made choices in the past that made sense at the time according to the knowledge that you had and the state of mind you were in at that time. Forgive yourself. You were doing the best you could. That is all anyone ever does. Don't let the *if only* thoughts hijack your mind and take over your emotions. Accept the past for what it was and move forward.

Making friends with your past is not the same as repressing it or never thinking about it. It's allowing yourself to think of the past in healthy ways. Remember the happy times, and ponder the lessons you have learned along the way. But have no regrets. Regrets are a train of thought that leads to suffering.

Lesson #30:

Thinking about what should have or could have been is a seed of regret and unhappiness.

Exercise:

Is there something in your past that you regret? Write down what you remember about the event. Then read through it to see if there is a lesson you can learn. Sometimes the lesson is more than what you would do differently in hindsight. Some lessons provide a greater understanding about yourself and how you react in certain situations. Self-awareness is a powerful lesson. Be grateful for these lessons. Then let it go. You may wish perform a mini ceremony to symbolize the release of the regret. I like to write it all out on paper and then throw it in a fire. As the paper burns, it symbolizes the release of the regret. As the smoke is rising, repeat this affirmation: "I am grateful for the lessons I've learned from this experience." This is a very empowering act. Deal with one regret at a time, and be patient as you move into a more forgiving and grateful relationship with your past.

~ 31 ~

Avoiding Arguments

"When an argument flares up, the wise man quenches it with silence."
~ Ralph Waldo Emerson

"Everything that irritates us about others can lead us to
an understanding of ourselves." ~ Carl Jung

"Where did you put my keys?" Does this sound familiar? One person gets frustrated because he can't find something, then he starts yelling at another to release the anger by blaming that person. The important thing is to bring awareness into the situation. If you are the one who is frustrated, as soon as you are aware of your irritation take a few deep breaths and then nicely ask for help finding your item. If you are the one being yelled at, take a slow, deep breath and remind yourself that it isn't personal. Offer to help without arguing back. When we allow ourselves to blame others or feel like we need to defend ourselves from being blamed, we fuel the fire of a potential argument. Blaming others is ego based, as well as defending yourself against verbal attacks. Somehow, the ego thinks that by blaming others it releases themselves from responsibility. It doesn't. It just satisfies the need to feel justified in taking their frustration out on others. Basically, it's an unaware mind letting off steam.

It is challenging on both ends, because it is most likely a repetitive behavior on both parts. Either way, it is a wonderful opportunity to practice self-control and awareness. Whichever part you play, do not let it spiral into an argument. Learning to respond to minor irritations without amplifying the frustration will avoid many arguments. Speak your mind when it is important and necessary, but let the little things go. This may seem trivial, but I assure you that it is in conquering the small challenges in life you will gain the most personal power and happiness.

Lesson #31:

Learn to hold your tongue to avert minor arguments.

Exercise:

The next time you are in a situation where either you or someone you are with is frustrated, take a slow, deep breath. This will give you a moment to respond with awareness.

Bringing awareness to the situation gives you the power to control your emotions, which in turn usually has a calming effect on the other person. With awareness you have the opportunity to respond with patience and understanding instead of the normal reaction of mirroring the frustration. It takes two to argue but only one to diffuse a situation before it explodes into an argument.

~ 32 ~

Be Balanced

"Throw moderation to the winds and the greatest pleasures
bring the greatest pains." ~ Democritus

"The happiness of a man in this life does not consist in the absence,
but in the mastery of his passions." ~ Alfred, Lord Tennyson

The world is full of ups and downs as the pendulum of life swings back and forth. These swings are beyond our control. With awareness we can see the swing of the pendulum and ride out the extremes. But with our personal choices, we have the power to be more balanced. Maintaining balance as much as possible makes life easier to handle. It's like the difference between riding a roller coaster and riding on a slow, level train ride.

When we indulge ourselves with extreme behavior, it usually has undesirable consequences. Too much unhealthy food yields obesity and the health issues that come along with it. Too little food and you become malnourished, sickly, and weak. Just the right balance, and you enjoy good physical health. It is the same for most everything we do in life. Too much of a good thing is not a good thing. We must become aware of how our personal choices affect our life. Too much work, you become stressed and your personal relationships can become strained. Too little work, and you might not be able to support yourself and your family. Life is about balance. If your life is a pie chart, when you indulge too much in one or two sections of the pie then the other sections grow smaller and will show signs of neglect.

Lesson #32:

Maintain balance and moderation in all things.

Exercise:

This is an awareness exercise. Become aware of what needs balancing in your life.

Take a piece of paper and evaluate how much time and attention you give to the following, listing the activities you do in each section of your life. Add to or change the example list to reflect your life:

- Physical well-being: health and fitness activities, your dietary habits.
- Emotional well-being: relaxation, playing, taking time for yourself, reflecting life lessons.
- Relationships: spending time and attention with people who are important to you.
- Spiritual growth: spiritual practices, meditation, prayer, service.
- Finances: work, financial planning, budgeting.
- Mental growth: learning something new, reading, puzzles, etc.
- Creative endeavors: Expressing your inner artist, gardening, redecorating, building something, music, arts.
- Life experiences: Your bucket list, things you really want to experience.

Not everything will be equal, nor should it be. Some areas of life will take up more time than others. The point of this exercise is to raise your awareness of where your time and attention are at this time. Reflect on the areas that might need more time and attention, evaluating if you should pay more attention to them. Reflect on your two most time-consuming areas. Are you paying too much time and attention on these and neglecting other areas of your life? Only you can answer these questions. Every life is different. And each year of your life may have a different focus. Your life should be an expression of what you feel is important. It should reflect your authentic self. Just make sure that you aware of what matters to you, then enjoy it all in a balanced way.

~ 33 ~

Be Who You Are

"There is a part of every living thing
that wants to become itself:
the tadpole into the frog,
the chrysalis into the butterfly,
a damaged human being into a whole one.
That is spirituality."
~ Ellen Bass

A girl asks her Grandmother, "How do you know what your purpose in life is?"

The grandmother gently takes the child by the hand and leads her toward a pond where a frog is sitting on a lily pad.

Grandmother says, "Dear little one, see this frog? Does he have to think about what his purpose is before he sits in the sun to warm himself or swims with delight with his friends? Does he think about being patient and working hard for his next meal as he awaits a passing fly?"

The girl responds, "I guess he just does those things naturally, Grandma."

"Yes, and by following his instincts and doing what he naturally yearns to do, he is living his life's purpose."

You too might wonder if there is a purpose for your life. I assure you that there is. Finding that purpose is part of discovering your authentic self. The more you align yourself with who you really are, the clearer your life purpose will become. Finding yourself involves listening to your intuition and your natural instincts. If you yearn to play piano or find yourself composing original melodies in your head, then the chances are good that your life purpose involves music. When we suppress our basic natures or our inborn talents, we are holding ourselves back from being all that we could be. When we suppress our innate yearnings of self-expression, we suppress a huge part of who we are. This can result in feelings of uselessness, low self-esteem, and depression.

Finding your life purpose involves moving beyond your childhood programming and following what feels right to you. If you are in a family of doctors and were always expected to grow up to be a doctor, this may or may not be in alignment with who you really are. Only you can answer the call of spirit, which will guide you to express your innate gifts. By allowing your innermost desires of self-expression to come out, you release yourself from being who and what everyone else thinks you should be, thus finding yourself in the process.

> *"It isn't until you come to a spiritual understanding of who you are—not necessarily a religious feeling, but deep down, the spirit within- that you can begin to take control." ~ Oprah Winfrey*

Not everyone's life purpose will be an enormous influence on the world, such as Oprah Winfrey, Bill Gates, and Gandhi. Sometimes your life purpose is felt most on your inner circle of family and friends. *But the most important result of living your life with purpose is the effect it has on you. You will feel immense passion and joy for life.* Also, by being authentic to who you are, you will inspire others to be themselves too.

Act in alignment with your heart and connect with spirit, and you will be living your life with purpose.

Lesson #33:

The purpose of life is to reconnect with your authentic self and then to let your life be an expression of who you are.

Exercise:

Do you act in alignment with your authentic self, your deepest desires, and your intuition?

The best way to decide if you are living your life with purpose is how you feel about who you are and what you do with your time. It's not about thinking or logically planning a life of accomplishments. Finding your self is about connecting to the still small voice of spirit in your heart. It's about listening to your intuition and instincts. It's about rediscovering the pieces of yourself that may have been lost or suppressed. Sit quietly and take a few deep breaths. Take a few minutes to really feel who you are.

What it is that you wish to do, to experience, to express, to be like today, next week, next year?

This is the most important question you will ever answer. The answer will change over time as you continually evaluate your innermost desires. The purpose of life is to connect with your authentic self and then let your life be an expression of who you are. Once you know who you are, you can evaluate what is working in your life to achieve balance between who you are and how you live. Evaluate what is in alignment with your dream of self-expression.

Do you believe and think you are on the path to actively live out your sense of self?

Do your words and actions work for or against your authentic self?

Find a way to act and speak in alignment with who you are and what you want to experience.

Realize your dreams of self-expression by:
- Realizing what they are.

- Believing you can reach them by being yourself.
- Keep doing what works. Stop what isn't working.
- Follow a path of action in alignment with your dreams.

Be true to yourself and you will be following your life purpose.

~ 34 ~

Unconditional Giving

"When you give your heart receives." ~ *Rosemary Smith*

*"You can easily judge the character of a man by how he treats
those who can do nothing for him.* ~*Malcolm Forbes*

A grandmother and her young granddaughter are walking down a busy city street. They pass by a homeless man. He is sitting against the granite wall of a high-rise building. The man doesn't have a sign or a cup for begging; he is busily making roses from palm leaves. There are two roses beside him. The grandmother stops and asks if she could buy one of the roses. The homeless man smiles and says, "For you, kind lady, it is free." The grandmother takes out her purse and gives the homeless man five dollars. As they walk away, the young girl asks her grandmother, "Why did you give him money? He will probably just buy beer and cigarettes." The grandmother replies, "Dear one, it may be his nature to take the money and buy beer and cigarettes, but it is my nature to give to a man in need."

When we give from our loving nature, not from our ego, we have no conditions or expectations. We give because it is our loving nature to do so. If we give with conditions and expectations of how the gift should be used, or think that others should give equally in return, we are setting ourselves up for possible disappointment. Giving with conditions is an ego-based activity. It is not based from your heart but from a need to control others.

It is not always the gifts of money and things that we tend to give with conditions. Many times it is our time, attention, and love that come with strings attached. You may not be aware of it, but this is very common in relationships. When someone is lacking in his sense of self-worth, he often looks to fill it with someone else. He gives his love and attention, expecting that it will be returned in kind. He is giving of himself with conditions of getting something he needs in return. This is a recipe for resentment in a relationship. It becomes a tally of who owes who. Love because it is your nature to love. Love for love's sake. Love because it opens your heart, not because you need or expect something in return.

Lesson #34:

Give without expectations or without conditions. Give because it is your nature, not because you want something in return.

Exercise:

Become aware of your motives for giving. Honestly ask yourself if you give to others because of what they can give in return or because you are giving from your heart.

This is a self awareness exercise. It may take time to honestly assess yourself. Do not judge your patterns of being. Become aware of them, and then you will have the power to choose differently. Awareness always brings free will instead of the same old reactive patterns.

~ 35 ~

Open Your Heart

*"Only the development of compassion and understanding for others
can bring us the tranquility and happiness we all seek."*
~ Dalai Lama

"Be kind, for everyone you meet is fighting a hard battle." ~Plato

Do you have compassion? Compassion is when we open our hearts to empathize and extend love to others. It may be easy to have compassion on those you see as suffering from life events or forces outside themselves, but can you offer compassion for those who are victims of their own poor choices. Can you have compassion for a crack addict as well as a baby born with health issues? Can you come to a place of compassion for those who are stuck in unawareness, suffering in a living hell of their own doing? If you can have compassion on all who suffer, regardless of the cause of suffering, then this is unconditional compassion.

Unconditional compassion is nonjudgmental. It comes from a fully open heart. The more open your heart is, the more love you will be able to give and the more love you will be able to feel. A heart with conditional compassion is limited in its ability to fully feel love. The heart becomes blocked. The blockages in a heart are a result of the ego mind pushing for separation from others and spirit. The ego has to justify its existence through thoughts of self-righteousness and an *I'm better than you* attitude. These types of trains of thought lead to justification of conditional compassion, which in turn limits our expression of love.

Practice feeling compassion toward those you normally judge as *losers*. The reality is they are suffering because they have lost themselves. Thoughts of judgment only serve to irritate us and reinforce feelings of being better than others. Praying for those who suffer will not only help them, it will enhance your own feelings of serenity and begin to clear away any blockages in your heart. An open heart is able to freely express love to others and feel the immense joy of receiving love.

Lesson #35:

Practicing unconditional compassion opens your heart, which enables you to fully express and feel love.

Exercise:

Become aware of any instances where you are reluctant to feel compassion for someone who is suffering, *regardless of the cause of the suffering*. When you find yourself resisting real compassion, say a prayer for the person. Pray that his or her suffering will soon be over. Pray for your heart to open wider and to have compassion on all beings.

~ 36 ~

Bring Back the Family Dinner

"It's not the taste of the food, the time it took to make it, or the clean up at the end that I remember. It's the warmth of family and friends, all coming together, like a communion of souls." ~ Memories of Wednesday night dinners

One simple step to enjoying life is getting together with other people to share a delicious meal. This used to be the norm in most households. Families would eat together at dinnertime, sharing experiences of their day, elders passing down stories and wisdom to the younger generation. When I was growing up, we ate breakfast and dinner together on most days. When I had children of my own, I made it a point to have most dinners together as a family. The television was off, and the conversations were on!

Family gatherings, which are the birthday parties, big Saturday or Sunday dinners, holiday feasts, and such are also a dying art of human socializing. My husband's family of eleven children used to have a Sunday dinner at the Grandma's house every week. Of course, this is back when people would actually take one day off a week to be with their family and friends, connect with God, and spend time in nature. Our culture is becoming so overcomplicated that people are forgetting how to just relax and be with each other without outside distractions and entertainment.

The memories of the Wednesday night dinners are my own. For ten years, when I lived in Rhode Island, I would host a Wednesday night dinner for family and friends. My husband would pick up his blind nephew from the group home, I would fetch Grandma, and sometimes four or five friends would show up. Even my teenage son would sit with us during the simple meatball and spaghetti meal. These simple dinners fostered relationships and created memories that we all share to this day. It wasn't always easy or convenient, but we did it. I can honestly say it was worth the effort.

If you make it a priority, you can bring back the family dinner. It takes a bit more scheduling, but people always make time for what they really want to do in life. I think this is one of those things worth making an effort to do on a regular basis. Make a habit of sharing at least one meal a day with family or friends. It builds stronger bonds and makes a lifetime of memories.

Lesson #36:

Gathering for meals with family and friends on a regular basis fosters closer relationships.

Exercise:

Take responsibility to bring back the family dinner in your life. Make a habit of regularly sharing meals and time with people who you care about or those you would like to have closer relationships. Whether you can gather together daily, weekly, or even monthly, the result will be quality time spent together creating shared memories. Sharing time dining together is one very simple step to building better relationships. It offers an opportunity to communicate and to be with each other. Build some happy memories- bring back the family dinner.

~ 37 ~

Avoid Poisoning Yourself

"He who conquers others is strong; he who conquers himself is mighty." ~ Lao Tsu

If someone offered you a bottle of poison, would you willingly take possession of it, and then carry it around so you could take a sip once in a while? Many people do this all the time with emotional bottles of poison. When someone insults you, puts you down, or ridicules you, it is emotional poison. If you walk away with those toxic thoughts in your head, you take the poison with you.

Every time you think about it, you are taking a sip of poison that destroys your peace of mind and lowers your self-esteem. To avoid carrying around these poison thoughts, do *not* take possession of them. You take possession of them by paying attention to them in the first place. If someone tries to poison your mind with insults, ignore the statements, because any defense just gives it more attention and power over you. *What you do not acknowledge as an attack, you need not defend.* Walk away from it and think of it no more. The bottle of poison isn't yours unless you claim it as such. No one has the power to hurt us with their words, unless we give them the power by planting their poison weeds in our head.

Lesson #37:

If you take no offense from others, you need not defend anything.

Exercise:

The next time you are in a situation where poisonous statements are being thrown at you, remember your ABCs of responding to life. Take a slow deep breath. This will give you a moment to remind yourself that you need not defend anything. You can ignore the statement. Realize that when other people are spouting poison, they are unhappy people expressing their low self-confidence. They don't realize that putting others down makes them look petty and judgmental. The important part is that you come to realize that you cannot be harmed by other people's words unless you agree with them.

This exercise will be challenging at first. It is not easy to give up a lifetime of taking every insult personally. By becoming aware of the situation when it is happening, you are raising your self awareness. As you have more self awareness, discovering how you normally react in certain situations, you will gain the ability to choose a different response. Raising awareness always raises your free will, because you will see different choices. Be patient with yourself as you practice not defending yourself and taking what others say personally.

~ 38 ~

Be a Cheerleader

"Note how good you feel after you have encouraged someone else.
No other argument is necessary to suggest that you never miss
the opportunity to give encouragement." ~ George Adams

Be a cheerleader! You can be a positive force in the world. Begin being a cheerleader to those around you, especially those who need a boost of self-confidence. Support people's dreams with excitement and encouragement. It is when you believe in others that you will have the courage to believe in yourself. When people accomplish something, applaud their efforts. When something wonderful happens to them, be happy with them. Being a cheerleader opens your heart, allowing you to feel the joy along with them.

Now that you are learning to pay attention to the positive aspects of life instead of focusing on the negativity in the world, you will naturally become a positive influence on those around you. Everyone needs someone to believe in their dreams and to coax them on when they are ready to give up. You can be that person. When people express their hopes and dreams, don't shoot them down with doubts or reasons why they shouldn't pursue them. Stand up and say, "Good for you! I believe you can do it!"

Instead of looking at the whys, look at the why-nots. Allow others to pursue their own lives in their own way. Everyone looks for validation in one way or another. They want to know that their lives have meaning, that what they do is noticed by others. They want you to say, "I see you. You matter." You can be that person. When we offer encouragement to others, it not only gives them a boost of self-confidence, but it promotes a warm feeling in our heart. Being positive is beneficial for everyone.

Lesson #38:

Being positive is beneficial for everyone.

Exercise:

Let others know that you see them and that they matter to you. Let them know that you support their dreams. Give honest compliments when the opportunity arises. When you send positive energy out into the world, it will be reflected back to you. By helping others to build their self-confidence, you will be increasing the positivity around you. It is much easier to maintain a positive outlook when you are surrounded by positive people.

Begin your cheerleader training. Practice giving honest compliments and words of encouragement. It acknowledges their efforts, accomplishments, and the positive aspects of who they are. When you practice being a cheerleader, spreading positive energy will become a habit. It only takes one person to start making a happier world. That person is you.

~ 39 ~

Personal Freedom

"Do one thing every day that scares you."
~ Eleanor Roosevelt

There are many other boxes that people tend to live in besides the physical structures. There are numerous mental boxes of which you will need to become aware of to be free. Some of these mental boxes are connected to your definition of self. Perhaps you consider yourself to be quiet, reserved, or shy. These are boxes in which you feel comfortable, yet they are restricting you and your happiness nonetheless. Whenever we label ourselves, we put ourselves in a box.

It's time to break out of your box! Conquer fear, do something new, something that pushes you outside your comfort zone. When you break out of your box, you push beyond self-limitations, regaining personal power and freeing yourself in the process.

When we avoid doing things that are new and different, we remain inside our comfort zone. This may feel safe, but it limits our experiences. When you push yourself into doing something you normally would never do, it is an act of personal freedom. It doesn't have to be a big change to reap a big reward. Even the smallest act of freedom will effectively decrease your self-limitations and increase your personal comfort zone.

The biggest act of freedom for me was overcoming my fear of the ocean. I used to be afraid of sharks, so I would never go past my knees in the Gulf of Mexico near my home. I had convinced myself that since there were indeed sharks in this area, that it wasn't safe to swim over my head. This was a senseless fear because very rarely is anyone attacked here. I decided to conquer this fear by swimming out to a buoy that was thirty yards from shore. I stood at the water's edge for a few minutes, pondering my fear and my chances of swimming there and back without getting attacked. Finally, I started walking into the water. I was almost halfway there, waist deep, when the most unexpected thing happened. As I continued walking I began walking up hill. By the time I reached the buoy, I was in two feet of water while standing on a sand bar! I laughed out loud at my self, realizing the phobia was unwarranted, and had been holding me back from swimming.

All these years, I never knew that my fear of swimming to that buoy was actually a fear of nothing. I realized that it was the fear itself that had paralyzed me. I regained so much power from that experience that I can now swim without anxiety, and I enjoy snorkeling. I would be missing so much if I hadn't taken that first step outside my box.

Another fear I had was to sing karaoke in front of people. I would get anxiety whenever I went to karaoke with my friends, fearing that they would push me to sing with them. After a year of going out to karaoke, I finally got the courage to face my fear. I sang. When I finished, I had a rush of personal power. I felt relieved and excited. I now sing anywhere, anytime I can. I think back to how scared I used to be, still in my box of limitations, and am so grateful that I pushed out of my comfort zone.

When we fight our fears, we are fighting our ego. Ego has a set of rules that it likes to follow, making sure that it remains in power. It convinces you that change is bad, makes you think about what other people think of you, and generally needs to keep you living in fear to maintain control. When you argue for your limitations, it keeps you boxed in, a prisoner of your own fear of being free. Push yourself to do something new whenever you have a chance. Or be proactive by setting up personal challenges to conquer your fears. The freer you are, the more passion for life you will feel.

Lesson #39:

Moving out of your comfort zone and doing something that scares you will increase your personal power.

Exercise:

You can start by pushing yourself in small ways—perhaps trying a new food or singing karaoke. One of my favorites is wearing silly hats. Change how you normally dress, or change your hair. If you are an extrovert, try being quiet. If you are an introvert, become the life of the party. Challenge yourself to push beyond your self-limitations. What can you do today that you've been afraid to do? Successful completion of freedom challenges will give you more personal power and a bit of excitement too. Have fun!

~ 40 ~

Sing and Dance

"Dance as though no one is watching you.
Love as though you have never been hurt before.
Sing as though no one can hear you.
Live as though heaven is on Earth."
~Father Alfred D'Souza

Singing and dancing are excellent activities to promote presence. Both can be used as a mode to clear your mind of unwanted trains of thought. Additionally, for some people, singing and dancing can be acts of personal freedom. If you are not a singer or dancer, it would be a great idea to start breaking out of your box with these activities.

Singing is an instant mood enhancer. When you sing, it increases your oxygen intake, which makes you feel more energized. The deep breaths and consciously controlled diaphragm movements exercise your lungs and abdominal muscles. The act of singing requires your attention to regulate your tone, rhythm, and volume. This effectively keeps your mind on the present moment, which eliminates any other trains of thought. If you need a quick pick-me-up, sing a few songs out loud. You will feel more energized both mentally and physically.

Dancing is another good activity to focus your attention on the present moment. When you dance, you are busy concentrating on the way your body is moving to the rhythm of the music, and sometimes you are coordinating your moves with a partner at the same time. Dancing is a wonderful form of exercise. Exercise helps elevate moods because of the increased oxygen intake and the release of the body's natural mood-enhancing hormones.

Dancing allows the outward expression of the joy of life. When we dance, we energize our spirits with the rhythmic movements of the body. This allows built-up stress to be released and be replaced with a feeling of exuberance and peace.

Once, while watching the sunset over the Gulf of Mexico, I witnessed the most amazing sight. The sunset is always beautiful, but what captured my attention was a girl dancing. She was running, jumping, and pirouetting with such excitement. This little girl really knew how to express her enjoyment of life and nature. There were no self-conscious thoughts of what people were thinking of her while she danced. It was pure happiness in full expression. Dancing is one of the most natural modes of joyful expression.

Lesson #40:

Singing and dancing are both excellent mood-enhancing and stress-relieving activities.

Exercise:

When you have an opportunity to sing and dance, do you? Or do you choose not to because you are self-conscious? Don't let your fear of being heard or seen stop you from enjoying these wonderful activities. If you are one who avoids these simple pleasures of life, then it is time to break out of your comfort zone and move into the wondrous happy zone of musical expression. The next time you have an opportunity to sing or dance, do it. You will be amazed at how wonderful you will feel by performing this natural expression of life.

Sing, sing a song. Make it happy, make it strong …

Sing in the shower.

Sing in the car.

Sing at church.

Sing in glee club.

Sing to yourself.

Sing to the world.
Sing in your office.
Just sing!

Dance in the rain.
Dance with others.
Dance at home by yourself.
Dance in the park.
Dance in your office.
Dance at weddings.
Dance under the moonlight.
Dance to the rising sun.
Just dance!

Making singing and dancing a habit is one simple step to enjoying life.

~ 41 ~

Planning for the Future

Each night, they passively sleep with serenity,
unscathed by the shadows of life's worries,
unlike men, who so often choose to suffocate themselves,
drowning nightly in the waters of their dark speculations.

"Flowers" from *Awakening Perception*

Let's discuss the future. The future is not now, yet on a practical level it deserves some consideration in the now. It's not necessary to dwell on tomorrow too much, but you do need to have some sort of clue as to what you are doing today, next week, and next year.

Planning for the future, scheduling small tasks, appointments, and goals, is an important part of being a functional adult. Especially in today's society, it has become necessary to organize and prioritize life at least to some extent. There's nothing wrong with planning. Planning has its purpose. Thinking about the future is part of being a human.

The problem for unhappy people is too much thinking about the future in negative ways. When you worry about what may happen later today, tomorrow, and next year, you are focusing on what you do not want to occur. Most of the time these scenarios never play out. By worrying, unhappy people occupy their minds with negative thoughts, which creates anxiety. They worry about every little thing, making themselves nervous wrecks.

Worrying about the future is just as unproductive as dwelling on the past. There's nothing you can do about the past; it was as it was. In the same way, the future will unfold as it will, with or without your worrying.

That doesn't mean that you shouldn't plan and be prepared for life. Be proactive. Do what you can to anticipate life and drive yourself toward your dreams. But let go of those thoughts that needlessly focus on undesired outcomes. When you worry, you are preoccupying your mind with thoughts that generate anxiety, which results in stress. If you find yourself worrying, gently bring yourself into the present. Evaluate the concern you were thinking about and decide if there is something that you can do to prevent the undesired outcome. If you can be proactive, do it! And then let the situation go. Remember Lesson #21: Worrying is a waste of mental energy and destroys peace of mind. Don't allow the worrying thoughts to take over your mind and hijack your emotions.

Since we live in a busy world, there are usually numerous activities that need to be scheduled in the near future. Set aside time to prioritize and schedule your life. It probably won't take more than fifteen minutes of your day. You can use this time to do all the thinking and planning for the next day. Once this is accomplished, it will be easier to push the worrying aside.

Many people find it helpful to address their following day's agenda before they go to bed. If you have a clear picture of what your schedule will be tomorrow, you will sleep better. There will be no reason to lie awake worrying or even just thinking about all the tasks that need to get done. Do not attempt to keep your entire life scheduled in your head. Use a calendar, appointment book, or a PDA. Once you write it down, you will be able to let the thoughts go. There will be no reason to think about it anymore. The important tasks will be scheduled and you will think about them when the time comes.

Lesson #41:

Too much time spent thinking about the future will result in needless worrying. Schedule your life outside your head.

Exercise:

It's time to stop worrying and over thinking about everything you need to do. This week, start using an appointment book or another form of agenda. Take a few minutes before bed to look over the next day so you know what the plans are when you wake up. Then have a restful night.

If you catch yourself worrying, gently bring yourself back to the present moment. Take a deep breath. Evaluate the worry. Is it something you can take action to prevent? If so, then do it. If not, then it's time to let the thoughts flow through and out of your mind. Keep your attention on the now. Enjoy your time without worry.

~ 42 ~

Embrace Your Beauty

"A woman whose smile is open and whose expression is glad has a kind of beauty no matter what she wears." ~Anne Roiphe

"In so much as love grows in you, so in you beauty grows."
~St. Augustine

Beauty is a cultural agreement of what physical traits are most desirable. To evaluate yourself on external criteria that are beyond your control is to sentence yourself to a life of trying to mold yourself into an ideal of what is currently considered beautiful. This type of behavior reinforces low self-worth by repeating thoughts that you are not good enough the way you are. It drives people to have unnecessary cosmetic surgery and to develop hate for their own natural physical characteristics.

Real beauty comes in all shapes, ages, colors, cultures, and every other variety imaginable. There is nothing more attractive than self-confidence mixed with compassion, or a warm, authentic smile. Realize that *beautiful* isn't an adjective but an action verb. It is an expression of being. Act beautiful by being loving and compassionate. Act beautiful by being an expression of joy to those around you. Be an example to others. Stop trying to mold yourself into the media's idea of beauty and embrace your own beautiful traits as the uniqueness that is part of what makes you you. Real beauty comes from within.

Even those of us who have fended off the peer pressure of culturally conforming to current beauty standards can be surprisingly affected by loss of youth. You may feel less than you used to be because the years have etched a few lines on your face or you no longer have the body of a twenty-year-old. Real beauty comes from the charisma and radiance of self-confidence and inner joy. It never matters how old you are. Age is a number. The higher the number, the more you have experienced and the wiser you become. Don't let growing older be a cause of distress. Let each year be a badge of honor you display gracefully. (And remember to stretch!)

Fluffy or thin, old or young, wrinkle free or etched to perfection, love yourself. You are perfectly beautiful just the way you are!

Lesson #42:

Realize that beautiful isn't an adjective but an action verb. It is an expression of being.

Exercise:

Make a list of what makes you beautiful as a person. Start each sentence with "I am beautiful …"

Examples:

I am beautiful when I help others.

I am beautiful when I smile.

I am beautiful when I play with my dog.

I am beautiful when I embrace who I am with love.

Realize that beautiful isn't an adjective but an action verb. It is an expression of being. Be real. Be beautiful.

~ 43 ~

Love Yourself First

"Love yourself first and everything else falls into line." ~ Lucille Ball

"You are valuable just because you exist. Not because of what you do, or what you become." ~ Max Lucado

Don't confuse the desire to share your time and love with another person with the need to complete yourself or feel whole. When people convince themselves that they are incomplete without being with another person, they are deluding themselves into thinking that somehow another person can make them feel whole. No one can make you feel happy or whole. These are feelings that can only come from within your own heart.

Sure, a new love will provide feelings of elation and a temporary feeling of fulfillment, but as the newness wears off in the relationship so will the feeling of completeness, unless you have learned to love yourself. The void you may feel in your heart is because you haven't embraced your own perfection. Love yourself first and then you will be offering a complete person with a whole heart to the relationship. This is why before starting any new relationship it is important to work on your relationship with yourself first. Until you truly embrace who you are and love yourself, despite the imperfections of being human, you won't be ready to have a relationship that isn't based on neediness.

It can be challenging to overcome a lifetime of self-judgment. Be gentle with yourself. I use a positive affirmation every morning to remind myself that "I am healthy, happy, and whole." Whenever I feel self-doubt, I repeat this phrase a few times. It may sound like it won't make a difference, but I assure you that it will. Loving yourself first is a fundamental step to being happy.

Self-love is not selfish. When you embrace all that you are, loving yourself with all of your heart, it is an act of personal healing and a step toward feeling whole. This is not an act of selfishness, for selfishness is an act of holding onto that which you fear to lose or acting without regard for other people. True self-love is recognizing your self-worth, and when you feel your own self-worth you will naturally see the worth in others. How you feel about yourself is mirrored onto others. Having self-love allows you to forgive not only your own mistakes but everyone else's too. Believe that you are perfect just as you are today, even if you decide on a new definition of perfection tomorrow.

Lesson #43:

Love yourself first, then you will have a healthy and whole heart ready to love the world!

Exercise:

Begin to build your self-love by taking care of yourself. Make time for yourself to relax and rejuvenate. Treat yourself to a pedicure or a massage. Do something more for yourself than you usually do. You might want to prepare a special favorite meal. Treat yourself like you would treat your best friend or your spouse. It is time to put yourself first until you can honestly say that you love yourself and deserve to be treated as well as you treat others. You must heal yourself before you can be a happy, whole person for everyone else. You deserve as much love as you have ever felt for anyone else. Embrace who you are. Then you will be ready to share your love in a healthy way, not a needy way.

~ 44 ~

Relationships

"Shared joy is double joy. Shared sorrow is half a sorrow." ~ *Swedish proverb*

"What you leave behind is not what is engraved in stone monuments, but what is woven into the lives of others." ~*Pericles*

People need people. It is our bonds of interconnection that create unity. Well adjusted people reach out to others in both loving service *and* when they are in need of assistance. Interdependence is the highest form of social well-being. It pushes beyond the isolation of independence and brings in a healthy dose of interconnection. Happy people make an effort to connect with people. All it takes is to lend an ear, be a friend, or share something of yourself with someone. You strengthen relationships by giving them your time and attention.

People bond with others through shared experiences, mutual affection, and common interests. When you share your time with someone, giving them your full attention, it creates an emotional connection. People may forget what you have talked about. They might even forget things you do for them, but they will never forget how they feel around you when you acknowledge them with your attention. Let them know you *see* them. If you want to make a lasting impression on someone, open your heart, listen to them when they speak, look them in the eyes, give encouragement, and always offer hugs when appropriate. Some people go a whole day or more without experiencing the touch of another human being. Even a pat of the shoulder or back can long be remembered and appreciated. Be generous with your hugs and attention. A genuine hug expresses more love than a thousand words.

Learn to be a good listener. When we actively listen, we are paying attention to what people are trying to communicate. Often we can be caught up in our own thoughts and not really be paying attention to what others are saying. Sometimes you just don't think that what others are telling you is important. Be aware of this tendency and start to listen more. You may be surprised to find that when you actively listen, you can learn something from the most unexpected sources. It never ceases to amaze me that when I take the time to really pay attention to people, I see them as my teachers, and the lessons they are offering become clear.

In every life, there are a few essential relationships. These are your lug nuts. If you were an automobile tire rim, you would have five very important lug nuts keeping you balanced. These lug nuts are your inner circle of family and friends. These are the people who encourage you to follow your dreams and interact with you on a regular basis. They offer emotional support and are a major part of your life. The lug nuts are the ones who will answer the phone at 3:00 a.m. if you call and will be there to help you move. They are your best friends and closest family. Without lug nuts, your life could become off balanced. Lug nuts are an essential part of life.

The tire in this analogy represents everyone else. The tires will last for a time but are replaced many times over a lifetime. These are the numerous acquaintances and extended relatives who come in and out of your life. They usually serve a purpose for a time and then are replaced as they naturally fall away from your life.

Sometimes our strongest bonds are with our friends. Friends, unlike family, have been carefully selected to share in your life. Real friends will always support your dreams with encouragement and bring a smile when you need it, ever bringing light into your life. They will laugh and cry with you. They will allow you to experience who you are by not trying to change you.

One of the most important lessons that life has taught me is to see the beauty in everyone. Some people will teach you to develop characteristics that you admire in them. Others will teach you to soften the traits that you dislike. And a few will teach you that it is perfectly okay to be who you are, because they are comfortable with themselves. Open your vision to see these values and you will honor every relationship.

Lesson #44:

Learn to see the beauty in everyone. Every relationship is a gift. Every person you meet is a teacher.

Exercise:

Who are your lug nuts? Evaluate how many strong relationships you have in your life. Name five of the closest relationships you have. If some are in need of strengthening, it is easily done with your time and attention. Relationships are built on shared experiences, strengthened by your attention, and essential to a healthy happy life.

Plan to spend time with the people that are important to you. Listen more than you talk. Be as much a friend as you would like them to be for you. Let them know, above all, that you *see* them. Let them know that they matter to you. And give them a big hug!

Practice seeing everyone as a teacher. Whether you like him or her or not, you can learn something about yourself through the relationship. Raise your awareness and learn to see the lessons in every relationship.

~ 45 ~

The Joy of Service

"Many times when we take the focus off of ourselves and work to help others, our own problems shrink in size." ~ Angie Hoover Lawson

Being of service to others is one of the most powerful techniques to raise your spirits. When we are helping others, it takes the focus off our own problems while building a sense of self-worth. It also arouses feelings of interconnection and love. Since love is the master from which all positive emotions spring forth, it will trump all negative emotions. If you feel awful and don't know what else to do, after you pray for peace of mind, go help someone. You will feel like you make a difference. It will remind you that what you do matters. At the same time, it will refocus your attention away from your own personal problems. Serving others always allows us to build and strengthen our bonds of interconnection.

I remember the night I learned of my daughter's death. I was emotionally stunned and just sat looking out the front window all night. As morning came, I noticed the man across the street come outside to pick up his garbage, which had been spread all over the place by some animals overnight. Without thought, I went outside and started helping him pick up the garbage. We didn't speak, and he had no knowledge of what I was going through. When we were done, he said, "Thanks." and went back inside. It was those three or four minutes, picking up garbage, that were the most peaceful moments of that day. Acting in service, even in one of my darkest moments, helped me feel at peace for a few minutes. So yes, service will not only help others, it will help yourself too.

Lesson #45:

Being of service to others is one of the most powerful techniques to raise your spirits.

Exercise:

Do you feel overwhelmed with your own problems? Or feel like you're in a funk? Offer to help someone in need. Become aware of when people could use some help. There are so many opportunities to be of service. It can be as simple as giving someone a ride to the store or offering to do yard work for the old widow next door. Even just bringing someone a warm meal or a plate of cookies can make his or her whole day brighter. When we pay attention to the needs of others, we're not only helping them, we are helping ourselves in the process. It opens our heart, which allows us to feel more love. An open heart is a healthier and happier heart.

Lift the spirits of two people. Give someone a helping hand today! If enough people make a habit of helping others, it will be a kinder world. It starts with you.

~ 46 ~

Forgiving Is a One-Person Act

"To forgive is to set a prisoner free and discover that the prisoner was you."
~ Lewis Smedes

Who do you need to forgive in order to release yourself from the prison of repetitive emotional pain? How long will you hold onto this pain like a deluded victim clinging to the knife that stabs him, pretending that you aren't the one wielding the weapon? Forgiving is a one-person act. It never has anything to do with the person we hold resentment or anger toward. *It has to do with our attachment to the anger and resentment.*

To forgive, we must first release the desire to justify holding onto the anger and resentment. Instead of telling yourself all the reasons that you should be angry and resentful, tell yourself that you deserve to have peace of mind. *When we stop justifying our pain, it loses its attraction.* Then, you can see the cause of your suffering for what it is: a destructive train of thought.

Again, forgiving is a one-person act. Forgiveness never has anything to do with the other person. It does not condone whatever actions or words hurt you. It is making a decision not to let the event keep hurting you over and over. It is an act of self-healing. By releasing the thoughts of resentment and anger, we release our attachment to suffering.

Some people think that you shouldn't forgive someone unless he deserves to be forgiven. This is not being fair to yourself. You are the one who deserves to be free of this heavy weight. If you think you need to wait until the other person apologizes or somehow repents, you have given him the power over your suffering. Don't let others control your emotions. Remember lesson #17: *You are responsible for how you respond to people and events in life.* You are the only one who can end this suffering. You are not doing him a favor by forgiving. You are releasing yourself from the bondage he holds over you. The act of forgiveness releases you from the repetitive thoughts of being a victim. You may have been hurt once, but until you forgive and let those thoughts of resentment go, you will be a victim of this emotional suffering again and again.

Once you forgive a person, it does not mean that you should allow the same situation to repeat itself. Just because you have forgiven something, it does not mean it is okay to allow it to happen again. Be forgiving in nature, but be wise in your decisions to interact with others by not playing a fool. Forgiving doesn't necessarily mean that the relationship should return to what it was. Sometimes it will be even better, sometimes it will change as new boundaries are set, and sometimes it completely ends. No matter how the relationship changes, the important part is that you aren't suffering with anger and resentment anymore.

The act of forgiveness may take time, so be gentle with yourself as you move toward breaking free from this dark prison.

Luke 6:28 says, "Bless them that curse you, and pray for them which despitefully use you."

The advice given here is the key to releasing any resentment in your heart that you may be holding . When we become attached to our emotional pain, we resist letting go of it. This causes suffering. By praying for those who act in unawareness, we are not only helping them with our prayers, we are helping to heal our own hearts. There is no need to carry this pain and resentment anymore. Pray for those who have hurt you. Stop clinging to the pain.

Lesson #46:

Forgiving is a one-person act.

Exercise:

Is there someone you need to forgive to release the emotional pain you feel? Think of this person. Imagine him standing in front of you. Imagine that there are visible strings of attachment. The more emotion you feel, the more strings you should imagine. Imagine that you have a pair of scissors in your hand. Take the scissors and cut a string as you say, "I release my attachment to you. Many blessings to you that you may also heal." Imagine that as you cut the string, it springs back into you and they move farther away from you. The string represents your emotional energy that has been tied to this person, and when you release it you regain personal power that was lost. Continue this healing meditation as long as you have strings to cut or as long as you feel comfortable. Repeat this meditation as many times as you need to completely cut all strings of emotional attachment. This may seem like it wouldn't do much, but I assure you that this is a powerful healing meditation that will help you to release yourself from suffering.

Many blessings to you as you regain your personal power and release your emotional suffering. Be patient, with awareness and the intent to let the anger and resentment go, you will be able to forgive anything.

~ 47 ~

Dare to Dream

Perhaps destiny is an unchangeable seed,
as an acorn can be naught but an oak tree.
Yet, maybe fate is only a default design,
the shape of its growth in our own mind.

Perhaps destiny is woven in such a way
which allows our inner intentions to sway
the ultimate path which the branches will take,
each branch a choice that free will makes.

"Seeds of Destiny" from *Awakening Perception*

Ayoung girl said, "Grandmother, I'm scared. How am I going to know how to be an adult? How will I become wise like you, to teach my children and grandchildren? I'm afraid I'll never be able to learn everything I need to know. There is so much I don't understand."

Grandmother took her little hand in hers and led her to a small sapling apple tree that was no taller than she. "Look at this tiny tree," Grandmother said. "Right now it is young, it doesn't provide much shade, and it is too young to produce fruit. What do you think will happen to the tree over the next twenty years?"

The child replied, "It will grow into a big tree with lots of fruit."

"Ah, my child, you are already gaining wisdom. You can see that its destiny is to grow into a mature tree and to produce the fruit of its nature. So it is the same for you. Your destiny is to gradually grow into the wise, wonderful woman that you desire to be, for that is your nature."

And so it is the same for our dreams. Never think that a dream is too big or too difficult to accomplish. Once you set your heart's desire and intend to follow a dream, you have set your destiny upon the path of fruition. Most dreams are accomplished gradually, one step at a time. The only fear you should have is giving up your dreams.

Nike said it best: "Just do it!" Start by taking a small step. You don't have to know every detail along the way when you first start. Keep your focus on what you need to do first, and possibly second, and the rest of the journey will unfold as you go. It's like driving at night. You don't need to keep your eyes focused on more than what your lights are shining on just ahead of you. As you move along, you will see what direction you need to steer. Paradoxically, although you should keep your focus on the steps in front of you, always keep the bigger dream vision alive in your mind. Don't try to imagine all the details of the journey. Just keep a firm vision of what the end will look like and what the end will *feel* like. Believe in your dreams, feel your dreams, and they will manifest.

It is wise to periodically reevaluate what direction your life is going. Are you in alignment with your desired dream of life? Set clear intentions and then keep your actions and words aligned with your goal, as these are the steps on the path. Change directions and dreams as often as you like, but always be aware of where you're going. And above all, enjoy the journey!

Lesson #47:

Dream big! Your dreams will guide your actions of today and forge your destiny of tomorrow.

Exercise:

Ben Franklin said, "God helps those who help themselves." We can dream all day and pray all night, but without using our free will to act in alignment with our dreams, we will go nowhere. It's like saying you want to lose weight but not changing how you eat, or saying that you wish you were closer to your children but not scheduling time to be with them.

You can think of a thousand reasons not to take the first step, but it takes only one action to begin. Just one action that is aligned with your dream will get you on your way!

What small step can you take today to better align yourself with your dream of life?

~ 48 ~

The Power of Silence

Look inward, you'll find the beauty of your soul.
Look outward, you'll find the beauty of this world.
But it's when you're still and seek nothing
that you'll find wholeness.

"The Power of Silence"

In Eastern cultures, it is a part of growing up. Their children are taught and regularly practice meditation to calm the soul and connect with spirit. They understand the value and necessity of calming the body and mind for mental health. The importance of balance is well understood and actively practiced.

Our culture bombards us with audiovisual stimuli and adds the stress of over scheduled agendas. Too much mental and physical activity drowns out our still small voices of intuition and keeps us disconnected from spirit. It is important to take a few minutes every day to just *be*. In the sounds of silence, you will hear your heart sing and feel the calming stillness of inner peace.

Silence …

quietly sings
breathes peace
frees thought
brings release

Silence …

connects one
to the source
allows unity
guides course

Silence …

relaxes mind
clears chatter
relieves worry
so fears shatter

Silence …

charges soul
renews self
taps knowledge
of innate wealth

"Silence" from *Awakening Perception*

Lesson #48:

Taking time every day to silence the body and mind is an essential step to inner peace.

Exercise:

Remember Lesson #5: *Consciously breathing is one of the most important tools for self-awareness, transformation, and stress relief.*

Take a few minutes everyday to be silent. Sit or lie still, relaxing your body. Breathe deeply and slowly. Concentrate on how your body feels as you embrace the silence. Try the following simple breathing exercise.

1. Inhale slowly to the count of five, filling your lungs as much as possible. Feel your lungs expand. Visualize healing energy coming into your body. Concentrate on your breath as it fills your body with oxygenating life force.
2. Hold the breath for a count of three.
3. Exhale slowly to the count of five, squeezing every bit of air out. Feel your muscles contract to expel the air. Visualize releasing toxins from your body. Feel the stress leaving your body as you exhale.
4. Hold for the count of three.
5. Repeat at least ten times.
6. For a more advanced technique, slow the inhale and exhale to a higher count, or increase the number of repetitions for a longer meditation.

Relax, breathe deeply, and you will feel rejuvenated.

You can do this simple stress-relieving exercise any time you feel overwhelmed or just want to reconnect with spirit. Even just a few minutes will help regain emotional and spiritual balance. Start practicing this simple meditation every day, and you will begin to embrace silence as your sanctuary. Practice being a human *being*, not a human *thinking*.

~ 49 ~

See No Evil, Hear No Evil,
Speak No Evil

"The soul, like the body, lives by what it feeds on."
~J. G. Holland

By this point, you have certainly realized the connection between what you think about and your emotional state of mind. You have been becoming more aware of what you talk about, how you react versus respond to situations, and overall how to pay attention to the more positive aspects of life. It will be a lot easier to keep your mind clear of negative thoughts if you can keep the initial seeds of negativity out of your awareness in the first place. To do this, you must analyze the sorts of visual and auditory input that you subject yourself to on a daily basis. Do you listen to gossip and drama-filled stories about other people? Do you watch slasher movies where people are being hurt and murdered? Do you spend hours every day watching the news?

The news is a conglomeration of all the most sensational negative happenings around your part of the world, all presented to you in an audiovisual presentation that is designed to hook your attention in order to get high ratings. What is the news anyway? According to dictionary. com, *news* is a report of recent events in a newspaper, on the radio, or on television. Out of all the recent events that have taken place, only the most extreme, most negative, and most shocking will be highlighted on the news. This isn't a balanced picture of the world. It focuses on grabbing your attention in order to get ratings so that the TV networks can sell advertising for more money. It's a business. The news as it is reported today is not a seed of happiness. It will disturb you. It will germinate in your thoughts to the point where you feel the need to share it with others just to relieve the negative tension.

There is no need to completely cut off your media intake. Just become aware of the overabundance of negativity that you are putting into your thoughts and limit your news intake to the minimal. I've found that by going to the Internet for news I can discriminate which stories I want to explore in more detail and effectively ignore most of the sensationalized shock stories. By controlling what I hear, see, and read, I am able to focus on more uplifting current events. I do read most of the headlines, so I'm aware of the major happenings in the world. I just don't overindulge in tragic events and other upsetting stories. I live with acceptance that bad things happen in this world, I choose to focus beyond them and pay attention to more uplifting happenings.

See No Evil, Hear No Evil

Honestly evaluate what you feed your mind every day. Every source of input you allow into your mind will become a seed of thought. That is how advertising works. Businesses bombard you with the same ads over and over until you are brainwashed into buying their products. Life in general is the same way, filled with sensory input. When you repetitively focus on something, it will sway your thoughts, which in turn affects your moods. What you choose to pay attention to feeds your mind. If you are feeding it an overabundance of pointless drama (reality TV), negative conversations (gossip and complaints), and meaningless distractions (video games), then the result will be a life of drama, negativity, and meaninglessness.

Be aware that what you watch on TV, what you spend your time talking about, and what types of posts you allow in your Facebook news feed will have an overall effect on your mental state of mind. If you watch horror TV (too much news, shows with violence) then you are filling your mind with images and drama that may come back to haunt you with unhappy trains of thought. If you get involved with gossipy conversations, those drama-filled thoughts will be circling around in your head, urging you to share the gossip with others. If your Facebook news feed is filled with people who post negative content on a regular basis, such as complaining about life or other people, this will disturb your peace of mind. *It is easier to regulate what you are feeding your mind than to eliminate the unhappy or disturbing thoughts once they have been put there.*

You are in control of what you feed your mind. If you want to be happier and enjoy a life of meaning, then begin feeding your spirit with more uplifting input. Forget reality TV and come back to your own reality. Take time to see and hear your natural environment. Pay attention to the people in the room with you. Turn off the TV and computer, make plans with people you enjoy being around, laugh until it hurts your cheeks, and make some happy memories. Start on a diet of positivity and you will see amazing results.

Speak No Evil

When we speak ill, gossip, and pass judgment on others, we only hurt ourselves. It demonstrates a lack of compassion, intolerance, and pettiness, which diminishes our character. Gossiping about others spreads seeds of disharmony. It perpetuates stories that are usually negative and often built on misconceptions and lies. Do not involve yourself in these types of conversations. It will only contribute to upsetting your peace of mind and degrading your own character.

Lesson #49:

See no evil, hear no evil, speak no evil.

Exercise:

Pay attention to what you are feeding your mind. What types of things do you watch, listen to, and read? Make a point to move your audiovisual input toward more positive input. You feed your body every day. Make it a priority to also feed your mind. Read uplifting and spiritual material. Listen to inspirational people. Watch comedies instead of tragedies. Stop feeding your soul a junk–food diet and give it some real nourishment.

Become aware of how damaging gossip is to people. It disturbs happiness and makes the gossiper seem petty and judgmental. Make a promise to yourself to be no part of any gossipy conversation. You will feel much better about yourself if you speak no evil. Practice directing conversations away from gossip. Be an example to those around you, showing them that you don't have to talk about other people. As an unknown sage once said:

Great minds talk about ideas.
Average minds talk about events.
Small minds talk about people.

~ 50 ~

Eat with Awareness

A plump orange sphere
fills my hand as I gently twist,
falling free from tethered tree,
taste buds juice with anticipation,
fingers peel as fragrant droplets mist,
passionately, both hands grasp,
separating, revealing delicious flesh.
O, God, thank you, for breakfast!

"Florida Breakfast"

I often enjoy dining at a local sushi bar with a good friend. Every bite explodes in my mouth with such perfection. We both use this time to eat with awareness and laugh as we moan, "Mm, this is so good!" Besides the joy of the experience, when you savor your food you eat slower, which results in eating less. Learning to savor your food is something you can enjoy every time you eat.

One of the simplest joys in life is eating, yet we often miss this opportunity because our minds are somewhere else. Pay attention to the unique textures, delicious aromas, and savory flavors. To really experience the joy of eating, you need to eat slowly, turn off the TV, and tune in to one of life's great pleasures!

First, if you are preparing your own food, take this time to appreciate the journey that the food has taken to arrive in your kitchen. Pay attention to the unique aromas and textures as you lovingly make your meal. Focus on how lovely the food will be on your plate, and imagine the wonderful taste of each dish.

When you're ready to eat, eliminate distractions like the TV. Create an environment that is soothing and pleasant. If you are dining with someone else, don't lose yourself in the conversation. Pause often to savor the eating experience with each bite. You can fully enjoy your meal and your delightful company. Just do each with awareness. This will naturally make you eat slower, which gives your brain a chance to realize that you are full, allowing you to stop before you overeat. Thus, eating with awareness aids in digestion and weight control.

Become aware of any mindless eating habits you may have. Common mindless eating scenarios are eating while watching TV, eating while working, or surfing the internet. When we eat in unawareness, we are not enjoying the food, and tend to mindlessly keep eating long after we are full.

Another part of eating with awareness is to consciously choose foods that promote health and well-being. You are what you eat, so be aware of your food choices and how they affect you physically and mentally. Some foods, like those high in sugar or complex carbohydrates, can drastically affect your moods as the glucose level in your body goes up and down. Become aware of how foods affect you and adjust your dietary selections accordingly. The healthier you eat, the better you will feel both physically and mentally. There are many sources to educate yourself about nutrition, but basically the more fresh fruits and vegetables you eat, especially when eaten raw, the more overall health benefits you will enjoy.

Lesson #50:

Eating with awareness is one simple step to enjoying life.

Exercises:

- Start to pay attention to how you feel after you eat certain foods. Adjust your diet as necessary to maintain a balance of health and nutrition. Incorporate more unprocessed and raw foods into your diet.

- Schedule one specially selected meal that you prepare for yourself. Choose healthy ingredients. Use the time of preparation to fully appreciate the opportunity to be able to eat this meal. This is a great gift. Not everyone in the world gets to eat every day, especially a meal like this. When you are eating, eat with awareness. Enjoy the meal like you have never eaten before. Learn to appreciate every bite.

- Be completely present as you peel and eat an orange. Enjoy the process of peeling, revealing the juicy flesh. Enjoy the sweet rush of flavor as each bite explodes in your mouth.

Eat slower and with awareness. Begin to savor your eating experiences. Pay attention to the aromas, textures, and flavors. Begin to enjoy the most tasteful part of life: eating! Bon appétit!

~ 51 ~

Be Patient

*"The essence of life is not in
the great victories and grand failures,
but in the simple joys."*
~ Jonathan Lockwood Huie

Patience is allowing life to unfold in its own time. If you feel the unease of impatience, bring your attention back to the present and remind yourself that there are no ordinary moments. Every minute of every day is just as fleeting and sacred as any other. Impatience devalues the present moment, as if it's not good enough. Become aware of this and start valuing all of your time.

Many of us have become so busy that we feel rushed and stressed throughout the day. Some of these feelings arise from the annoyance we cause ourselves by always waiting for the next activity. When you are in a mind-set of *waiting*, you are not present. If you are at a stop light, in a checkout line, or a doctor's office, you are in a traditional waiting situation. By switching your state of mind to being present, you can relax and enjoy these few minutes of inactivity. In a busy day, these moments give us a much needed opportunity to take a break.

Many people have experienced the agitation of waiting while stopped at a red light. For some reason, there seems to be a lack of acceptance when it comes to traffic. Logically, we know that red lights, detours, and accidents are a normal part of traffic. Yet when faced with a couple of minutes at a red light, some people feel irritated. They spend these couple of minutes dwelling on how long the lights are, how many lights are on their route, and how the car in front of them should have gone through the yellow light so that they could have sped through the light before it changed red. Sometimes they even start to verbalize derogatory names about other drivers. In these few minutes, instead of peace and relaxation, these drivers have worked themselves up into a fit of anger.

It's time to stop waiting and start relaxing. Use this time to take a few deep breaths, feel your body, hear the music of life, and be aware of the details around you. When you bring your attention to your physical body and the surrounding environment, you are forcing your awareness outside your head. This is an automatic tension reliever. Nothing can bother you when you are present in the moment.

Lesson #51:

Stop waiting and enjoy life as it is happening. Be where you are.

Exercise:

When you are in a waiting situation, give yourself a break!

Take a few deep breaths. Slowly inhale, feeling the air expand your lungs. Then feel the tension leave your body with each exhale.

Think an affirmation of gratitude for these few moments of tranquility that you are about to experience. *This is wonderful! I am so grateful for these few minutes of peace.*

Bring your attention to your surroundings. Engage your senses and be aware of sights, sounds, and smells. Get out of your head and reconnect with the world.

Start actively relaxing in situations where you would normally find yourself waiting. It's time to reclaim these precious minutes of your day! Begin to experience the peace and serenity that you can enjoy in these same few minutes. Cultivating patience is one simple step to enjoying life.

~ 52 ~

Surround Yourself with Serenity

Is your home or work desk a mess? Feeling that your living environment isn't quite as organized as you would like it to be is a personal call. Everyone has his or her own comfort level of tidiness. If your environment isn't aligned with your level of expectation, it can make you feel uncomfortable, scattered, and stressed.

Our living spaces are reflections of ourselves. When the mind is scattered, it flows out into the environment, manifesting as disorganization.

Everyone has his own level of comfort when dealing with how he keeps his environment. Some are perfectionists—one item out of place or one dirty dish will start the mind chatter. Others are more relaxed with how much clutter can accumulate before it bothers them. If it begins to bother you with mental chatter—"This is a mess. I really need to clean this. I hope no one comes over and see this mess"—then it's time to take action. If it is bothering *you*, then start to reorganize and freshen it up.

As your living environment begins to be more organized, your mind will feel more relaxed. If you can purge unnecessary items or too many objects you have been holding onto that represent memories from the past, you will feel a surge of freedom. When we hang onto objects, we invest some of our metal energy in emotional attachment. Whenever you can release these types of items, it is an act of healing and personal freedom.

Lesson #52:

Your living environment is a reflection of your state of mind. A soothing environment aids in calming your mind.

Exercise:

To regain comfort and peace in your living spaces, choose one small area where you spend a lot of time, and freshen it up by cleaning and organizing it. Reduce clutter and add peaceful items, such as fresh flowers, a water fountain, candles, pictures of loved ones, or anything else that soothes you. I have a salt rock lamp that I keep on my desk. I also enjoy lighting incense , candles, and listening to relaxing music. Try different methods to activate your senses of sight, smell, and sound.

Start small. Even one clean and calm area will make a difference in how you feel. Start with where ever you spend the most time. As you feel the resulting peace of mind and calmness, you will be encouraged to continue cleaning another day. Be patient with yourself as you move into a more peaceful environment.

~ 53 ~

Do You Always Have to Be Right?

"Confidence is being able to share your opinions;
Wisdom is not being attached to them."
~ LB Shannon

It is easy to get caught up in sharing your point of view with others. It's a natural mode of communication. I share what I think about a subject and you share your thoughts about the subject. This type of communication goes on all day long. While it can be quite pleasant to talk to someone who shares your view, it can be frustrating to talk to someone with an opposing view.

More often than not, unhappy people will hold on to their opinions to the point of arguing. They would rather be right than let it go. They have convinced themselves that if they can't get others to agree with them, they feel that their point of view is being threatened.

Agreement from other people is not necessary. Believe what you like, and let others do the same. Overly opinionated people haven't learned that when others have an opinion that may be different from theirs, it is the other person's right. They also haven't learned that it is perfectly normal for other people to have varying opinions about many aspects of life. This type of closed-minded approach to communication can result in pompous thoughts of being smarter than the other person: "Obviously they are wrong and are too stupid to see it." These thoughts of judgment, the aggravation, the bitterness that can arise from these confrontations is all because they had to show everyone that they were right. It was more important to be right than to be happy.

So how can we interact with others who have conflicting points of view from our own without conflict arising? It starts with being flexible with our own beliefs. Listen to their opinions. Ask questions like "Why do you think that is?" or "Where did you learn that?" The second key to interacting with opposing viewpoints is to understand that it is not always necessary to share your opposing thoughts. It isn't your job to teach everyone around you to see things like you do. It's okay to allow them to think differently than you do.

The most noticeable instances in my life concerning differing opinions are always politics. I've reached a point where I no longer put my two cents in these conversations. People are entitled to see the world from varying points of view, as each of us is unique in our perspective and life experiences. By not attempting to invalidate other's opinions, I maintain peace of mind among some very opinionated people. Sometimes I even listen and ask questions so that I can begin to understand why they see the world the way they do.

Example #1:

Joe: "I think the moon is a spaceship for Martians."

Mark: "That's an interesting point of view! What makes you think that?"

Joe: "My grandfather told me when I was young."

Mark: "Your grandfather sounds like an interesting guy. What else did he teach you?"

In this example, Joe shared an unpopular point of view about the moon. Instead of attempting to dispel Joe's belief, or belittle him for his belief, Mark chose not to challenge the point of view that the moon is a spaceship. Mark asked for more information about Joe's belief, which showed interest and also revealed the root of Joe's odd belief. When Mark heard that Joe's grandfather told him that the moon was a spaceship, he steered the conversation toward the grandfather. This technique of redirecting conversations is a useful tool for avoiding heated discussions when you come across a potential conflict of opinion.

Example #2:
Jane: "I can't believe you are still married to John after he cheated on you again!"
Mary: "It's understandable why you would feel that way. So how's the new job going?"

In this example, Jane shared her unsolicited opinion about Mary's marriage. Mary, in an attempt to avoid the subject, validated Jane's right to her opinion but neither agreed nor disagreed. Instead, she changed the subject. Mary knew that it wasn't necessary for her to defend her personal choices. She let Jane's comment go, not choosing to start a debate on the subject of marriage and infidelity.

It's not necessary to validate your actions and viewpoints to others. Be confident in your life choices and beliefs, but be willing to hear different points of view.

Lesson #53:

It is unnecessary to defend your point of view. Allow others the right to have their own opinions.

Exercises:
Ponder these questions. Be honest with yourself.
- Do you take yourself so serious that when you meet people with a difference of opinion you feel the need to set them straight?
- Do you feel irritated or even threatened by listening to opposing points of view?
- Is it your job to teach everyone to think like you do?

The next time someone shares an opinion or suggests an idea that is different from your own, see if you can resist the urge to share your point of view or push your own agenda. This exercise can be as simple as not being a backseat driver when someone else is driving or as challenging as listening to someone with a completely different political viewpoint.

Be aware of how it feels to rein in your ego. The uneasiness you feel is your ego fighting for control. As you practice ego awareness, it will become easier to recognize the ego's controlling manipulations and easier to ignore it. When you can come to a point of humility, not always having to prove your opinions and allowing others to have alternate views, it brings more peace to relationships and to your own mind.

Practice being an observer or a listener without getting into debates. Make an effort to hold your tongue without putting in your two-cents point of view, even if you think they are totally wrong. This is a valuable skill that will provide much less drama in your life.

~ 54 ~

When Your Cup Is Full, Stop Pouring!

"The key is not to prioritize what's on your schedule, but to schedule your priorities."
~ Stephen Covey

Time is a strange concept. It seems that most people live according to some sort of time schedule, usually attempting to squeeze in more time than there is. They say things like, "I don't have time" or "I wish there was more time." The problem isn't the amount of time in a day. Everyone has the same amount of time. The problem arises when people either agree to do too much because they have taken on more than they can handle or they don't schedule enough, not making the time for what is important to them.

Do you take on more than you can handle and then feel stressed? Do you have a problem saying "No" or try to please everyone all the time? Trying to do more than you can handle is like pouring hot coffee into a cup that is already full. If you keep pouring, it will burn you. It's all right to pace yourself, choosing to do what is important to you and not committing to everyone and everything that vies for your attention. Remember that if you are overworked and overstressed, then you won't be much good to anyone. Practice setting boundaries and limits on how many things you schedule, and then you will have time to drink that cup of coffee!

Take a look at your life. Is it over scheduled with activities to the point where you feel that you don't have time for self-improvement, creative endeavors, or quality time with loved ones? If you make a list of the top five priorities in your life, do you make time to attend to them? Decide what is important, schedule it, *and then* schedule the rest. You will be surprised at how much your life will be enhanced when you focus on what is truly important to you.

I periodically reevaluate my life and make a list of the five most important things to me. Right now, it's peace of mind, relationships, my dogs, writing, and spirituality. Because these things are a priority to me, I make time for them first. Then I schedule everything else. As time goes on, the priorities will change and so will my schedule of activities. It is impossible to do everything and be there for everyone all the time. You must become aware of your limitations, scheduling no more than you can comfortably handle. If you over-schedule, you will become tired and stressed, which makes everything in life less enjoyable. When you get so caught up in the multitude of activities that you have committed to, you may end up neglecting what is most important to you.

Lesson #54:

When your cup is full, stop pouring!

Exercise:

Evaluate your schedule, and ask yourself, "What is important to me?" Make time for what matters most to you, *and then* schedule the rest. If a relationship is important, then schedule quality time together. If it's your health, then schedule regular exercise routines and plan a healthy meal schedule. When you focus on what is important to you, you will feel at peace with your life and how you spend your time.

Do not take on more than you can handle in a balanced way. Taking on too much creates stress and imbalance in the rest of your life. Practice saying "No" when necessary.

Become aware of what is important to you, then make time for your priorities. Let the rest of your life be balanced with other activities that you have agreed to, but never more than you can comfortably handle.

~ 55 ~

You Never Have to Do Anything

Do you feel that there isn't enough free time in the day to do everything you'd like to do? Realize that everything you do is exactly what you have chosen to do, and therefore you should do it with all your heart. You have free will, but there is no *free* time—just time. You selectively decide what you are going to do with your time. You make agreements with yourself or someone else to do certain things at certain times. Then you can either spend your time in joyful awareness or spend it wishing you were doing something else. Wishing you were doing something else will build feelings of resentment. It's a matter of committing yourself to whatever you are doing at the time. You chose to do it. Either do it with joy or don't agree to do it in the first place.

I used to resent doing housework, especially washing the floors. Then I realized that I choose to do it, no one is forcing me to wash floors. I choose it because I want clean floors. Why should I resent doing something that I choose to do? Now I put the radio on and practice singing while washing. It becomes a joyful chore.

I often hear people complain about having to take care of their parents', grandparents', or children's needs. "I have to take Johnny to karate and then help him with homework. I have no time for myself." Well, actually, the time you have with Johnny in the car is time for building your relationship. The time you are waiting for his karate lesson is time you could be reading, meditating, going for a walk, or catching up on phone calls. The time you are helping with homework, you are fostering a better understanding of your child and nurturing his academic growth. What part of these examples is wasted time? All of it, if you are doing it with resentment in your heart.

Do you have a habit of saying that you *have to* do something, such as *I have to do the dishes, go to work, make dinner, clean the house,* or *give Grandma a ride*? When we phrase what we either need to do or choose to do with the wording *have to,* it brings thoughts of wishing you were doing something else, which can lead to feelings of resentment or just not enjoying the time spent doing it. Watch how you use this phrase and learn to say, *I choose to,* or *I'm going to,* which will keep your focus on free will. Or use my new favorite , "*I like to* clean my floors on Saturday." You are free to choose to enjoy whatever you do!

Lesson #55:

You never have to do anything. What you do with your time is your choice.

Exercise:

Become aware when you are wishing you were somewhere else or doing something else. Ask yourself why you are doing what you are doing instead of being where you are thinking about being instead. You made a choice. If it is something that you really do not want to do, then don't do it. Be honest. If you resent doing housework, then ask yourself why you do it. Perhaps you would rather hire a maid. Perhaps you would rather work out a different chore arrangement with the other people who live with you. Perhaps you will realize that you actually would rather do it yourself. If this is the case, do it with awareness and love. Practice being present. You may find that you enjoy it after all.

Be free to experience your time with awareness and joy. Don't be a victim of your ego mind telling you that you could be doing something else instead. These types of thoughts create unease and stress. Realize that you are free to spend your time however you choose. Time is always free. Are you?

~ 56 ~

Flow with Life

*"Cling not to the withered flowers of life. Keep only
the memory of their beauty in their prime."*
~ LB Shannon

Learning to flow with life is an important aspect to being happy. Each of us must learn to let go of anything, any habit, or anyone that no longer is in alignment with our innermost sense of being. Some things, situations, or people are purposeful for a time and then the cycle comes to an end. Just because it ends does not negate the meaning of what it was in its time, just as a beautiful annual flower will fade yet the memory of the beauty is what remains. And yet, even in death, flowers leave seeds for new growth. Such is the rhythm of life. People come and people go. This moment is here, and then it is gone.

We live in a dynamic universe where nothing ever stays the same. Life is never static; it's continually flowing with ups and downs like the ocean tides. When we fight the nature of these tides, we cause undue stress within our minds. Enjoy living in the present as it is, but don't get too attached to it, because life will be different soon enough. By riding on top of the waves instead of being swept up in the middle of them, we have the ability to steer ourselves along the wave. Learn to flow with the waves of life by riding the extremes with awareness and acceptance, or those waves will knock you down for sure.

Besides the tides of life, there is always an overall current that pushes you along. Learn to flow with life like water in a river. When rocks appear, effortlessly flow around the obstacles without even slowing down. The only dams you will encounter are the ones you build yourself: attempting to move against the current (trying to move backwards), getting stuck in a whirlpool (repeating the same mistakes over and over), or attempting to run off course (moving away from your authentic self). These movements are unnatural and filled with resistance. If you feel like your natural flow is off track, ask yourself if you are causing this resistance by choosing not to flow with life.

Remember to flow with the unexpected and enjoy the journey. After all, detours in life are the seeds of good stories!

Lesson #56:

Flow with life's tides and currents.

Exercise:

Practice flowing with the unexpected. Embrace life's detours. Detours aren't running off course. They are following the natural path of life, winding in unforeseen directions but still going with the flow. We can't always see every turn coming up, but we can enjoy the journey as life takes us through a different territory.

If you are someone who feels the tides of life as they rise high and fall low, be aware that they never stay high or low. It's just a matter of riding the tide with awareness. Don't let the low tides draw you down with them.

When you feel caught up in a low tide of your life, repeat this affirmation: "This too shall pass. Today, I will appreciate the serenity of ordinary moments and the powerful peace of higher awareness."

Stay aware and be patient, and your high tide will soon come.

~ 57 ~

Rising from Darkness

"Adversity is like a strong wind. It tears away from us all but the things that cannot be torn, so that we see ourselves as we really are." ~ *Arthur Golden*

In everyone's life, relationships will end, health may decline, and people will pass on. We all have to deal with loss and grief eventually. It is important to allow your emotions to flow, to allow yourself to feel any way that you feel, without judging or suppressing your emotions. Let the emotions flow, and then let them go. The sadness will eventually pass if you process the emotions with the knowledge that this too shall pass.

Part of being happy and enjoying life is learning to move through the low tides without getting stuck. Some people have a tendency to cling to loss much longer than is healthy. There may be thoughts of what-ifs, should-have-beens, or even blame. All of these thoughts are unhealthy and will not help you move out of the darkness. There are others who cling to their loss like a victim. They become attached to their pain. They think that by letting go of the emotional pain, they are dishonoring the relationship—as if by not feeling sad they are expressing to the world that the relationship wasn't that strong. These types of thoughts can keep them in the darkness for the rest of their lives. There is no dishonor in moving past grief and being happy again. When we cling to grief, we dishonor our own life and our own spirit.

I realized this after my eleven-year-old daughter, Nicole, died in 2000. There were times when my victim mentality would creep into my mind and tell me lies about how I should never be happy again. I came to the decision that the best way to honor her memory was to move forward and make the best of my life. It is then that instead of destroying my life, her death became a catalyst for personal transformation. It is in this way that your greatest loss can become your greatest gift. Allow yourself to move through it, instead of getting stuck in it or trying to forget it. Remember lesson #20: *What seems like a tragic circumstance can be used as a lesson to move you to a higher level of being.*

Many blessings to those of you in a low tide of life at this time. Please know that you can move through even the darkest time in your life, if you allow yourself.

Lesson #57:

You can move through even the darkest time in your life, if you allow yourself.

Exercise:

Ask yourself if you are emotionally stuck in the grief of a personal loss. If you are, begin to give yourself permission to move through the grief process toward a feeling of peace. Begin to believe that a devastating loss doesn't have to forever wound you. Begin to believe that you deserve to be happy again.

Make a conscious choice to steer your trains of thought toward the present and future when you find them focused on what you have lost.

You may find these affirmations helpful:

"It is okay to be happy again."

"I am more than my greatest loss."

"I am grateful for this opportunity to transform myself."

"What does not kill me makes me stronger and compels me to connect with who I am."

"God is always here to support and strengthen me."

~ 58 ~

Life Lessons

"You learn something every day if you pay attention."
~ Ray LeBlond

"Do what you like. Like what you do." I read this on a Life is good T-shirt tag. I have worn this T-shirt a hundred times, and until recently I never noticed this mighty message on the tiny tag. Life is the same way. Daily, we are surrounded by subtle messages that can guide us and teach us, but most of the time we aren't even paying attention enough to see or hear them. Life works in mysterious ways. Sometimes a word of wisdom is in the next song you hear on the car radio or a conversation you overhear at the checkout line in a supermarket.

By paying attention to your environment and the often overlooked details of life, you are not only raising your awareness but you are honing your ability to be present. This itself is worth the effort. But it is those subtle messages that seem to speak directly to me that always amazes me.

Life is an expression of our interconnections. Everything is interconnected. What one person does or says affects the rest of us. Spirit moves in subtle ways, guiding us to say things or to pay attention to something we may have missed. Learn to communicate with this form of spiritual guidance. Quiet your mind, and see what messages are there for you. I may see a dead squirrel in the road, reminding me to slow down and pay attention, which averts a potential accident. I may hear a song I have not heard since high school reminding me to call an old friend, who then tells me that she really needed to talk to me.

155

I am a student of life. I have studied different philosophies and followed many teachers, but life itself has been my best teacher. When I look for the lesson in a past experience, I always find one. Every experience in life has a lesson, even tragic experiences. If we suffer through something without learning in the process, then that would be a real tragedy. Don't play the victim. Learn your lessons and be stronger.

My experiences have given me precious knowledge about myself and the world. These life lessons have unlocked the door to who I am. When I need guidance or a nudge in the right direction, life always provides the perfect message. Pay attention, and see what life is telling you.

Lesson #58:

Life itself is one of the best teachers you will ever have. Learn to see the lessons it offers.

Exercise:

Practice paying attention to your surroundings. Look for the subtle messages in what you see and hear.

Take time to ponder the lessons of your past. Every relationship will teach you more about yourself. Raise your awareness by asking yourself the following questions. You may find it helpful to write your answers in a journal.

- What have you learned from your past experiences?
- What have you learned from your parents?
- What have you learned from your children?
- What have you learned from your most difficult relationships?
- What have you learned today?

~ 59 ~

Self-Awareness

*"What lies behind us and what lies before us are small
matters compared to what lies within us."*
~ Ralph Waldo Emerson

"What is necessary to change a person is to change his awareness of himself."
~ Abraham Maslow

Self-awareness is the cornerstone to transformation. If you do not understand yourself, how can you change?

One easy way to increase your self-awareness is to put yourself into an observational mode by watching how you usually react to people and situations. Bring your awareness into an observational mode by paying attention to your patterns of being and questioning your thoughts and behavior. You can then assess your behavior. Distinguish if the way you are acting is in alignment with who you desire to be. Do certain people seem to upset you or cause you to feel stressed? Discover what it is that you are thinking around them. Watch yourself and you will find out what situations push you into automatic reactions. Once you can recognize these situations, the mere fact of recognizing them brings a state of higher awareness. Then you will have the power to be however you choose to be instead of driving on impulse.

You may be surprised to find that when you come from a place of reaction, you are not in alignment with how you would choose to respond if you had given the situation a moment of thought. Once you have attained this watcher awareness, you will have the power to respond to life instead of operating with your automatic default reactions. Remember your ABCs of responding to life: Awareness, Breathe, Choose. Then you can choose love over fear, peace over conflict, and happiness over despair.

Lesson #59:

Watching how you interact in the world raises your self-awareness.

Exercise:

Practice observing yourself. Learn to shift your awareness as necessary. When you are watching yourself, you are in a state of higher awareness. In this mode of consciousness, you will be open to new types of behavior as well as increasing self-awareness.

Don't judge your efforts. Any amount of attention you give to this practice will enhance your ability to move into higher awareness at will. Have fun with this exercise. You will learn things you never knew about yourself.

~ 60 ~

Intuition

*"The intuitive mind is a sacred gift, and the rational
mind is its faithful servant. We have created a society that
honors the servant, but has forgotten the gift."*
~ Albert Einstein

Intuition is the spirit's way of communication. When we pay attention to our gut feelings we tune in to the direct perception of truth. Become aware of these types of sensations and follow your instincts. We were born with this sense of insight; we should learn to listen to it.

We are designed to be able to sense more than our primary five senses. If you have a gut feeling about something, it isn't your imagination, it is your intuition. Learn to pay attention to these feelings. Listen to your heart above all else, and you will discover a higher level of awareness.

Many years ago, I was driving home and I had this strong urge to pull into the grocery store and buy some groceries for a neighbor who I knew had been out of work for a few weeks with an injury. I purchased a few pounds of lunch-meat, some prepared salads, breads, and soda. I left them on her doorstep because she wasn't home. The next day, she told me about how her husband had died two days before and she had spent most of the day at the funeral home. She came home so tired and emotionally upset that she didn't have the energy to go out for food. She and her children had come home to the mysterious bags of groceries and were surprised and grateful to be able to make sandwiches. I had no idea that her husband had passed away. It was the still small voice of intuition that guided me to be the hand of spirit, helping them when they needed it.

The voice of intuition is that feeling you get out of nowhere, the urge to do something out of the ordinary, and the inner guidance that helps us when we need it. The voice speaks through the body. You will *feel* it. To understand its message, you must clear your mind and listen. By listening to the still small voice of spirit, you will be amazed at how life is enriched. Enhancing your spiritual connection will allow you to experience the mysteries and wonder of life. It activates your inner compass, allowing you to find direction and guidance when you need it. The next time you feel spirit calling, stop what you are doing, take a few deep breaths, and answer the call.

Lesson #60:

Learn to follow your intuition by feeling it.

Exercise:

Has intuition ever given you a message? If you are new to this concept, begin your practice by noticing when you feel a strange urge or have a thought that comes out of nowhere. The more you practice your intuitive skills, the better you will get at hearing and feeling them. Follow your intuition and see where it leads you.

~ 61 ~

Desire Less, Allow More

When we come from a mind-set of wants and desires, it can reinforce a lacking mentality. Constantly dwelling on your wants and desires instead of what you appreciate about your life right now causes disharmony in the mind. It is perfectly normal to dream of a future aligned with your innermost desires. As a matter of fact, it is essential to focus on dreams to manifest them. But it is when we are focused on the thoughts of dissatisfaction of today, based on the desire of the future, that our heads get filled with thoughts of lack.

When we come from a mind-set of being open and allowing, we are readying ourselves for action in alignment with our desires without the negative effect of a lacking mentality. It is a subtle difference of wording, but it makes a huge difference. For instance, one could say, "I want to be in better physical shape." This statement is one of desire but doesn't necessarily promote action, and it might create feelings of self-judgment for the shape your are in today. When reworded to say, "I am allowing myself to live a healthier lifestyle and become open to new physical activities," the stage is set for action which will produce desired results. Another example is this: "I want to find a nice man to date" versus "I am open to allowing a nice man to come into my life." That's it. Desire less; be open to allowing your dreams to manifest!

Lesson #61:

Desire less; allow more.

Exercise:

What are the things you typically would say you want out of life? Practice rewording those desires into statements of allowance. Write down all of your most powerful desires. Next to them, rewrite the desires into affirmations of allowing.

Start with this desire: "I want to be happy." Allow this: "I am allowing more joy into my life every day."

Post the new statements where you will see them often, to remind yourself to be open for your dreams to manifest.

~ 62 ~

The End Is the Beginning

You may have heard that there is a Mayan myth that the world will end December 21, 2012. Here are my thoughts: Who knows if it's true? I tend to think not, but if it is true, how would that knowledge affect your life today? Would you pay attention to the little things more: the birds chirping, the sun setting, your children vying for attention, and the taste and texture of your food? Would you offer forgiveness to those who you hold grudges and resentment against? Would you express your love more freely to those around you? Would you take time to pray, even though you may not ever pray? If so, why wait for your last day on earth to do these things? You may have one day left, or ten thousand. Either way, don't wait till the last minute to live in awareness, joy, and love.

Whether the world ends tomorrow, next year, or just ends for me when I die, I will not live any differently from how I do today. I am not afraid to die. I'm more afraid of not living while I'm alive.

Master Lesson:

Don't wait to live with awareness, joy, and love. Be happy now!

Exercise:

Imagine yourself many years from now in the last few minutes of your life. You are reflecting on the wonderful life you have had but also keenly aware of things you wish you had done differently, experiences you wish you had taken the time to enjoy, and people you wish you had shown more love and forgiveness. Sit quietly and ponder this for a few minutes.

Now imagine that magically you have a chance to go back to today and live out those years again, with enhanced awareness and with more love and unlimited joy. Poof! You are here, *now.* Be grateful for this second chance. Enjoy your life. It's a gift.

Be happy now!

Afterword

The purpose of this book is to share the lessons I have learned. By sharing the lessons I have gained, others may be able to raise their awareness and rediscover their authentic selves. These lessons are seeds of personal transformation. I may plant the seeds, but only you can make them grow. This is a book of knowledge. As such, you must question everything for yourself, for knowledge is just an interpretation of reality. Wisdom is when you apply the knowledge and find what works for you.

It is challenging to overcome a lifetime of unhappy habits. Many people spend years practicing these habits of complaining, being involved in drama-filled conversations, gossiping, worrying, regretting the past, feeling like a victim, and all the other dense weeds you must remove from your life. It will take some time to let new seeds of happiness grow. They will take root if you keep paying attention to them. And the stronger the seeds of happiness grow, the less the weeds will be able to survive. Your new habits of happiness will take the place of your old habits of unhappiness. Don't judge your progress. Any amount of attention you give these new habits will feed them. It won't take long. Before you know it, your life will start to be less stressful and more enjoyable.

If you read the book all at once, then I recommend going back to apply each lesson one at a time. Each exercise will raise your awareness and you will learn more about yourself in the process. You cannot read a book and become happier. But you can read a book, gain practical knowledge, and then apply it to your life, which in turn may transform you. These are the lessons that worked for me. You may find that these lessons work for you too. Take what you need and leave the rest.

"Knowing is not enough; we must apply.
Willing is not enough; we must do…"
~Johann Wolfgang van Goethe

Everyone has his or her own journey. Enjoy your journey of awakening. I wish each of you a life of joy and inner peace. Don't wait to live with awareness, love, and joy. Be happy now!

Namaste,

Laura Barrette Shannon

Lessons for Enjoying Life

Lesson #1: Your thoughts affect your emotions.

Lesson #2: Believe that you can live a life of joy and peace. Set the intent to be happy.

Lesson #3: You hold the key to your happiness, not special people, new things, or ideal life circumstances.

Lesson #4: You have the ability to bring your attention to the present moment.

Lesson #5: Consciously breathing is one of the most important tools for self-awareness, transformation, and stress relief.

Lesson #6: What you focus on affects your level of happiness or misery.

Lesson #7: By redirecting your attention, you have the ability to jump off negative trains of thought.

Lesson #8: Life won't always be what you think it should be. Accept it anyway.

Lesson #9: Become aware that complaining is a seed of discontent and unhappiness.

Lesson #10: You can't enjoy life if you are wishing you were someone else or focusing on a different time in your life.

Lesson #11: You can respond to life in a positive way. (Stop complaining.)

Lesson #12: You are the narrator of your life story. Make it a happy one!

Lesson #13: Be aware of how you talk about yourself. Words can either be empowering or victimizing.

Lesson #14: The world is a mirror. To change the way you see others, you must change the way you see yourself.

Lesson #15: Base your self-worth on your character, not on what you own, how much education you have, or your physical appearance.

Lesson #16: It is your responsibility to set the boundaries of how you allow other people to treat you.

Lesson #17: You are responsible for your interactions with people and your responses to situations in life.

Lesson #18: The attitude of gratitude will increase your happiness.

Lesson #19: Everyone has his or her own garden. Some are full of the weeds of stress and unhappiness. Don't let other people's weeds take root in your garden!

Lesson #20: What seems like a tragic circumstance can be used as a lesson to move you to a higher level of awareness.

Lesson #21: Worrying is a waste of mental energy and destroys peace of mind.

Lesson #22: Being hyper-focused on an activity can effectively stop negative trains of thought from circling in your mind.

Lesson #23: Emotional pain is like fire. When you direct attention its way, it fuels the fire.

Lesson #24: Reconnecting with your inner child makes life fun, full of wonder, and it expands time.

Lesson #25: Let emotions flow, and then let them go.

Lesson #26: Being with nature encourages presence, which reduces stress and rejuvenates the soul.

Lesson #27: The more you become aware of how you perceive the world, the more power you will have to change your perception to one more positive.

Lesson #28: Exercise helps elevate moods.

Lesson #29: Life is a personal journey of self-discovery. Allow others to have a chance to find themselves in their own way.

Lesson #30: Thinking about what should have or could have been is a seed of regret and unhappiness.

Lesson #31: Learn to hold your tongue to avert minor arguments.

Lesson #32: Maintain balance and moderation in all things.

Lesson #33: The purpose of life is to reconnect with your authentic self-and then to allow your life to be an expression of who you are.

Lesson #34: Give without expectations or without conditions. Give because it is your nature, not because you expect something in return.

Lesson #35: Practicing unconditional compassion opens your heart, which enables you to fully express and feel love.

Lesson #36: Gathering for meals with family and friends on a regular basis fosters closer relationships.

Lesson #37: If you take no offense from others, you need not defend anything.

Lesson #38: Being positive is beneficial for everyone.

Lesson #39: Moving out of your comfort zone and doing something that scares you will increase your personal power.

Lesson #40: Singing and dancing are both excellent mood-enhancing and stress-relieving activities.

Lesson #41: Too much time spent on thinking about the future will result in needless worrying. Schedule your life outside your head.

Lesson #42: Realize that beautiful isn't an adjective but an action verb. It is an expression of being.

Lesson #43: Love yourself first, and then you will have a healthy and whole heart ready to love the world.

Lesson #44: Learn to see the beauty in everyone. Every relationship is a gift. Every person you meet is a teacher.

Lesson #45: Being of service to others is one of the most powerful techniques to raise your spirits.

Lesson #46: Forgiving is a one-person act.

Lesson #47: Dream big! Your dreams will guide your actions of today and forge your destiny of tomorrow.

Lesson #48: Taking time every day to silence the body and mind is an essential step to inner peace.

Lesson #49: See no evil, hear no evil, speak no evil.

Lesson #50: Eating with awareness is one simple step to enjoying life.

Lesson #51: Stop waiting and enjoy life as it is happening. Be where you are.

Lesson #52: Your living environment is a reflection of your state of mind. A soothing environment aids in calming your mind.

Lesson #53: It is unnecessary to defend your point of view. Allow others the right to have their own opinions.

Lesson #54: When your cup is full, stop pouring!

Lesson #55: You never have to do anything. What you do with your time is a choice.

Lesson #56: Flow with life's tides and currents.

Lesson #57: You can move through even the darkest time in your life, if you allow yourself.

Lesson #58: Life itself is one of the best teachers you will ever have. Learn to see the lessons it offers.

Lesson #59: Watching how you interact in the world raises your self-awareness.

Lesson #60: Learn to follow your intuition by feeling it.

Lesson #61: Desire less; allow more.

Master Lesson: Don't wait to live with awareness, love, and joy. Be happy now!

Ten Quick Mood Enhancers

Smile. Studies have shown that the mere act of smiling actually fools the body into feeling happier. So fake it until you make it. Smile for no reason, and the smiles you get back will help to raise your spirits.

Take a shower. Water is naturally rejuvenating. It cleanses the mind and spirit as well as the body. If you are in a funk, take a long shower and you will immediately feel uplifted.

Take a walk. Taking a short walk will pep you up, release stress, and give you some exercise at the same time.

Sing a song. Singing increases oxygen, clears the mind, and makes you feel good.

Laugh out loud. Laughter feels good, reduces stress, and brings people closer together. Learn to laugh at yourself. Watch comedies, tell silly jokes, or just start laughing all by yourself for no reason.

Meditate. The calming effects of meditation are well known. Even a short five-minute breathing meditation will de-stress you and lift your mood.

Help someone. Helping others lifts the spirits of two people. Service is an act of spirituality.

Dance. Dancing is great for stress relief, getting the blood pumping, and expressing the joy of living.

Hug someone. When we share our loving energy with others, it is reflected back at us. Feel the love. Hug someone!

Stand tall. Did you know that the way you sit and stand can affect your mood? If you are hunched over with your head down and shoulders sagging, the chances are good that you are feeling unworthy, blue, or troubled. If you change your posture by keeping your shoulders back, head up, and back straight, you will not only start to appear more confident, you will feel it too.

The ABCs of Redirecting Attention

A: Awareness. When you become aware of a negative emotion you have gained the personal power to respond instead of react.

B: Breathe. Take a few slow, deep breaths. Feel the air move in and out of your body. Feel your muscles. Relax. This switches your awareness away from the charged emotion and into your body and the present moment.

C: Choose. Now that you have taken a moment to calm the emotion, you have the ability to choose an appropriate response.

Use the ABCs of responding to life, and you will feel less stressed and be in control of how you act and speak. Relax, breathe deeply, and be happy.

Resources and References

I recommend the following books and movies for additional study and inspiration. Each one helped to raise my awareness by planting seeds of emotional and spiritual growth. In this way, they made this book possible.

Allen, James, *As a Man Thinketh* (Tribeca Books, 2012)

Bennett-Goleman, Tara, *Emotional Alchemy: How the Mind Can Heal the Heart* (Harmony Books, 2001)

Covey, Stephen, 7 *Habits of Highly Effective People: Powerful Lessons in Personal Change* (Free Press, 2004)

Dyer, Dr Wayne W, *Change Your Thoughts - Change Your Life: Living the Wisdom of the Tao* (Hay House, 2007)

Dyer, Dr. Wayne W, *Inspiration: Your Ultimate Calling* (Hay House, 2007)

Emerson and Thoreau, *The Complete Works of Ralph Waldo Emerson and Henry David Thoreau* (CreateSpace, 2008)

Frankl, Viktor, *Man's Search for Meaning* (Beacon Press, 2006)

Gibran, Kahlil, *The Prophet* (Alfred A. Knopf, 1973)

Goleman, Daniel, *Emotional Intelligence: Why It Can Matter More than IQ* (Bantam, 1995)

Gregg, Susan, *Mastering the Toltec Way: A Daily Guide to Happiness, Freedom, and Joy* (Red Wheel/Weiser, 2003)

Millman, Dan, *No Ordinary Moments: A Peaceful Warrior's Guide to Daily Life* (HJ Kramer, 1992)

Millman, Dan, *Way of the Peaceful Warrior: A Book That Changes Lives* (HJ Kramer/New World Library, 2009)

Redfield, James, *Celestine Prophesy* (Warner Bros, Inc, 1997)

Ruiz, don Miguel, *The Four Agreements: A Practical Guide to Personal Freedom, A Toltec Wisdom Book* (Amber-Allen Publishing, 2001)

Ruiz, don Miguel, *The Mastery of Love: A Practical Guide to the Art of Relationships, A Toltec Wisdom Book* (Amber-Allen Publishing, 2002)

Shannon, Laura Barrette, *Awakening Perception: Poetry of a Toltec Warrior* (Xlibris Publishing, 2006)

Stephensen, Sean, *Get Off Your "But": How to End Self-Sabotage and Stand Up for Yourself* (Jossey-Bass, 2009)

Tenzin Gyatso, the XIVth Dalai Lama, *The Art of Happiness - a Handbook for Living* (Hodder, 1998)

Three Initiates, *The Kybalion: A Study of Hermetic Philosophy of Ancient Egypt and Greece* (Yogi Publication, 1905)

Tolle, Eckhart, *A New Earth* (Dutton Adult, 2005)

Tolle, Eckhart, *The Power of Now* (New World Library, 2004)

MOVIES:

Bucket List, Directed by Rob Reiner (Warner Home Video, 2008)

I Am, Directed by Tom Shadyac (Gaiam, 2012)

Miracle Worker, Directed by Arthur Penn (MGM, 1962)

Pay It Forward, Directed by Mimi Leder (Warner Home Video, 2001)

Peaceful Warrior, Directed by Victor Salva (NBC Universal, 2006)

Randy Pausch: The Last Lecture Classroom Edition, (Disney Educational Productions, 2008)

You Can Heal Your Life, The Movie, starring Louise Hay, Directed by Michael Goorjian, (Hay House, Inc, 2007)

About the Author

Laura Barrette Shannon is a poet, philosopher, and happiness coach. Her work includes the book *Awakening Perception* (2006) as well as the popular *Be Happy Now: Simple Steps to Enjoying Life* blog on Facebook.

Laura is a happy free spirit, despite life circumstances, having learned to rise above the loss of her daughter, cope with chronic pain, and successfully control her bipolar swings. When she is not writing, you may find her discussing philosophy at the park, watching butterflies in her backyard, or singing karaoke. She lives a life of joy and love with her husband and two dogs in Largo, Florida.